THE COMPLETE VEGETARIAN COOKBOOK

Chris Hardisty

TORMONT

CONTENTS

The publishers would like to thank the following people who supplied recipes and without whom this book would not have been possible: Chris Hardisty, Rosie Brook, Pam Knutson, Freda Hooker, Pauline Robertshaw, D.M. Arnot, Val Shaw, Brian Holmes, Vivien Margison, Isabel Wilson, Marianne Vaney, Ian Jones, Wendy Godden, Joan Davis, Jo Wright, Isabel Booth, Alison Ray, Susan Mills, Kate Allen, Pat McGlashen, Deirdre Kuntz, Suzanne Ross, Joan Davies, Merle Millan, Ann Bohren, Winifred Allen, Sumitra Gopal and Sally Halon.

Photography by Peter Barry
Food prepared and styled by Helen Burdett
Designed by Claire Leighton and Judith Chant
Typesetting and graphics by Julie Smith
Edited by Jillian Stewart
Cover design by Zapp

INTRODUCTION

There is nothing new or strange about vegetarianism. So many people have
adopted a vegetarian diet, whether for health or philosophical reasons, that this way of eating
has become commonplace. More restaurants than ever before have at least one vegetarian
main dish on the menu, and many have an entire vegetarian set menu, from appetizers
through to special desserts.

People come to vegetarianism for many different reasons – out of compassion for animals, or
through environmental and health concerns. For whatever reasons, vegetarians do not eat any
products derived directly or indirectly from the slaughter of animals, fish or birds, including by-
products like gelatin or lard. There are acceptable substitutes, though, that are easy to find in
supermarkets or health food stores, like agar agar, a gelling substance derived from seaweed that
substitutes for gelatin and works just as well as lard.

From the health point of view, vegetarians have lower rates of obesity and suffer less from
coronary heart disease, high blood pressure, cancer of the bowel and a host of other disorders
than meat eaters do. If you want to cut down on meat and animal products, include fresh
vegetables and fruit, plenty of bread, pasta, rice, grains, pulses and potatoes, and keep processed
foods to a minimum, a balanced vegetarian diet is just the thing. And if yours is a household
made up of both vegetarians and meat eaters, don't be surprised if the meat eaters want to
sample what you're eating, and then decide to have a "vegetarian day" now and again!

When protein requirements in a diet are based on meat, there are thousands of interesting protein
sources from around the world that get overlooked. Across the Far East, millions of people eat
nothing but vegetarian food, and many of the traditional African and Middle Eastern dishes are
meat-free, so you can add a whole new dimension to your diet simply by looking to the eating
habits of other countries.

Adopting a vegetarian diet doesn't mean eating endless bowls of muesli and millions of nut
burgers. As this book reveals, vegetarian eating is about imagination and experimentation,
diversity and change. You don't need meat for variety and with clever recipes, you won't even
miss it. You will notice, too, that none of these recipes rely on meat substitutes, like textured
vegetable protein. While there's certainly nothing wrong with these products, if you are going to
make the change to a vegetarian diet, why look for something that "tastes like meat." Why not
look at all the delicious ways you can eat without it!

SNACKS & APPETIZERS

Vegetarian snacks and appetizers offer endless opportunities for the cook to use his or her imaginative flair – whether it's a salad, stuffed vegetables, or a risotto, the scope is limitless. It is always best to look on any snack or appetizer as a mini main course where garnishing and presentation are concerned. This applies to the appetizer in particular, as it introduces the meal and should give a taste of things to come.

Appetizers can consist of almost anything you wish to serve, as long as the ingredients do not clash with the main course. Try to balance a substantial main course with a light appetizer and vice versa. Many main dishes can be served in small portions as appetizers or snacks so bear this in mind when searching through recipes. Pay attention to the ingredients and try not to duplicate them in the first course and main dish. For example, if your main dish is salad based, serve a hot appetizer such as soup.

Home-made soups are delicious, and as well as being the perfect first course, the heartier ones can be served with bread as a one-course meal. Making soup was once thought to be fiddly and time-consuming. Not so now with the aid of a food processor, although if you do not have one it is possible to press the soup through a strainer to produce a creamy texture. Most vegetables are suitable for use in soups, so this is a perfect way to use up almost any ingredients you have on hand. Soup also keeps well and often tastes better the day after it has been cooked!

FENNEL AND WALNUT SOUP

*A delicious and unusual combination makes this
soup perfect for special occasions.*

SERVES 4

1 bulb chopped fennel
1 head chopped celery
1 large onion, chopped
1 tbsp olive or sunflower oil
¾ cup walnuts, crushed
5 cups vegetable stock, bean
   stock or water
3 tbsps Pernod
⅔ cup cream
Salt and pepper
Parsley to garnish

1. Sauté the fennel, celery and onion in the oil over a low heat.

2. Add the walnuts and stock and simmer for half an hour.

3. Purée the simmered ingredients together and return to the pan.

4. Add the Pernod, cream and salt and pepper.

5. Reheat gently and serve garnished with parsley.

TIME: Preparation takes about 15 minutes, cooking takes about 1 hour 10 minutes.

SERVING IDEA: Celery leaves may be used as a garnish if no parsley is available.

VARIATION: Other nuts such as cashews or almonds may be used in place of walnuts. Use any aniseed-flavored liqueur in place of Pernod.

WATCHPOINT: Do not allow the soup to boil after adding the cream and Pernod.

CREAM OF CARROT SOUP

A classic soup which is suitable for any occasion.

SERVES 4

1 large onion, chopped
2 cloves garlic, crushed
1 tbsp olive oil
2½ cups carrots, chopped
1 tsp mixed herbs
3¾ cups stock
⅔ cup sour cream
Salt and pepper

1. Sauté the chopped onion and garlic in the oil until transparent.

2. Add the carrots, mixed herbs and stock.

3. Bring to the boil and simmer for about 30 minutes until the carrots are soft.

4. Cool a little and then blend until smooth.

5. Add the sour cream, season to taste and mix thoroughly.

6. Heat through gently and serve.

TIME: Preparation takes about 10 minutes, cooking takes 35 minutes.

WATCHPOINT: Do not allow the soup to boil after adding the sour cream.

VARIATION: For a richer soup, omit the sour cream and add a swirl of heavy cream just before serving.

WILD RICE SOUP

A meal in itself when served with whole-grain bread and a green salad.

SERVES 4

¼ cup wild rice
2 cups water
2 onions, chopped
1 tbsp butter or margarine
2 sticks celery, chopped
½ tsp dried thyme
½ tsp dried sage
3¾ cups water or vegetable stock
1 vegetable bouillon cube
1 tbsp shoyu (Japanese soy sauce)
6 small potatoes, peeled and roughly
 chopped
1 carrot, finely diced
Milk or cream

---

1. Add the wild rice to the water, bring to the boil, reduce the heat and simmer for 40-50 minutes until the rice has puffed and most of the liquid has been absorbed.

2. Sauté the onions in the butter until transparent.

3. Add the celery, thyme and sage, and cook for 5-10 minutes.

4. Add the water, bouillon cube, shoyu and potatoes.

5. Simmer for 20 minutes or until the potatoes are cooked.

6. Blend the mixture in a food processor until smooth.

7. Return to the pan, add the carrot and wild rice.

8. Add the milk or cream to thin the soup to the desired consistency.

9. Reheat gently and serve.

TIME: Preparation takes about 15 minutes. Cooking takes 30 minutes plus 40 minutes to cook the wild rice.

COOK'S TIP: You can prepare and cook the soup while the wild rice is cooking. Add the rice to the soup at the end of the cooking time.

FREEZING: Cook a large quantity of wild rice and freeze in small portions. Add to the soup or other dishes as needed.

VARIATION: Toast some sliced almonds and sprinkle on top of the soup before serving.

MISO SOUP

This delicious soup of Japanese origin makes a nice change as a first course.

SERVES 2

1 small onion, grated
¾-inch fresh root ginger, peeled
  and finely chopped
1 clove garlic, crushed
1 tbsp sesame oil
1 carrot, peeled and finely sliced
¼ small cauliflower, divided into florets
5 cups water
1 large tbsp arame (Japanese seaweed)
2 tbsps peas (fresh or frozen)
2 tbsps shoyu (Japanese soy sauce)
1 tbsp miso (red bean paste)
Black pepper to taste
2 green onions, finely chopped

1. Sauté the onion, ginger and garlic in the sesame oil for a few minutes.

2. Add the carrot and cauliflower and gently sweat the vegetables for 5 minutes

3. Add the water, arame, peas and shoyu. Cook for 15-20 minutes until the vegetables are soft.

4. Blend the miso to a paste with a little of the soup liquid and add to the soup but do not allow to boil.

5. Season with freshly ground black pepper to taste.

6. Serve garnished with chopped green onions.

TIME: Preparation takes 15 minutes, cooking takes 20 minutes.

SERVING IDEA: Serve with hot garlic bread.

VARIATION: Substitute other vegetables such as daikon radish, turnip, rutabaga, pea pods or green beans but remember that this soup is mainly a broth with a few floating vegetables.

COOK'S TIP: Arame, shoyu and miso are available from Japanese grocers, health food and other specialist food stores.

SPINACH AND APPLE SOUP

*The two main flavors complement each other
perfectly in this hearty soup.*

SERVES 4

2 tbsps butter or margarine
1 small onion, chopped
2 tbsps whole-wheat flour
2½ cups vegetable stock
1lb spinach, shredded
1 cup apple sauce
1¼ cups milk
Salt and freshly ground black pepper
Pinch of nutmeg
Lemon juice
Plain yogurt
A little parsley, finely chopped

1. Melt the butter in a large saucepan and fry the onion until soft.

2. Add the flour and cook to a roux.

3. Add the stock slowly, stir well and simmer for 10 minutes.

4. Add the spinach and cook until tender.

5. Cool slightly and mix in the apple sauce.

6. Place all the ingredients in a food processor and blend until smooth.

7. Return to the pan and reheat slowly together with the milk.

8. Add the salt, pepper, nutmeg and lemon juice to taste.

9. Serve in individual bowls with the yogurt swirled on the top and garnished with chopped parsley.

TIME: Preparation takes 15 minutes, cooking takes 15 minutes.

COOK'S TIP: The apple sauce can be omitted but it adds an unusual flavor to the soup.

VARIATION: If you have no vegetable stock available use a vegetable bouillon cube mixed with 2 cups of boiling water instead.

Easy Lentil Soup

*A good old-fashioned soup which is sure
to please all the family.*

SERVES 4-6

1 cup split red lentils
2 tbsps butter or margarine
1 medium onion, peeled and finely
   chopped
2 stalks celery, finely diced
2 carrots, scrubbed and finely diced
Grated rind of 1 lemon
5 cups vegetable stock
Salt and freshly ground black pepper

1. Pick over the lentils and remove any grit. Rinse well.

2. Heat the butter or margarine in a pan and sauté the onion for 2-3 minutes.

3. Add the diced celery and carrots and let the vegetables sweat for 5-10 minutes.

4. Stir in the lentils, add the lemon rind, stock and salt and pepper to taste.

5. Bring to the boil, reduce the heat and simmer for 15-20 minutes until the vegetables are tender.

6. Roughly blend the soup in a food processor – it should not be too smooth.

7. Check the seasoning and reheat gently.

TIME: Preparation takes about 10 minutes, cooking takes 15-20 minutes.

SERVING IDEA: Sprinkle with cheese and serve with hot toast.

FREEZING: Freeze for up to 3 months.

GARDEN VEGETABLE SOUP

A hearty soup perfect for those cold winter nights.

SERVES 4-6

1 tbsp margarine
½ head fennel, finely chopped
3 medium carrots, diced
1 medium onion, chopped
2-3 cloves garlic, crushed
1 parsnip, diced
Salt and pepper
2 heaped tsps dried parsley
1 tbsp tomato paste
1 large potato, diced
5 cups vegetable stock
⅓ cup frozen peas

1. Melt the margarine in a large pan and add the fennel, carrots, onion, garlic, parsnip and seasoning.

2. Cover and allow to "sweat" over a very low heat for 10-15 minutes, stirring occasionally.

3. Add the parsley, tomato paste, potato and stock.

4. Stir well, bring to the boil and simmer for 20-30 minutes until the vegetables are tender.

5. Just before serving, add the frozen peas.

6. Bring back to the boil and serve immediately.

TIME: Preparation takes 15 minutes, cooking takes about 35 minutes.

SERVING IDEA: Serve with crusty rolls or French bread.

VARIATION: If fennel is not available, use 2 or 3 sticks of finely chopped celery.

SPLIT PEA SOUP

*Reserve a few leek slices to garnish the top or
make it special with a swirl of yogurt.*
SERVES 6

1 cup split peas
1½ cups vegetable stock or water plus a
    bouillon cube
4 tbsps margarine
1 large onion, chopped
3 sticks celery, chopped
2 leeks, finely sliced
2 medium potatoes, peeled and diced
1 medium carrot, finely chopped,
Salt and pepper

1. Cook the peas in the stock for 10-15 minutes.

2. Meanwhile, melt the margarine and sauté the onion, celery and leeks for a few minutes.

3. Add to the peas and stock together with the potatoes and carrot and bring back to the boil.

4. Simmer for 30 minutes.

5. Season well and purée until smooth.

TIME: Preparation takes about 10 minutes, cooking takes 40 minutes.

SERVING IDEA: If the vegetables are chopped finely,
you can serve this as a chunky soup.

COOK'S TIP: If you do not have a food processor you can push the soup through a
strainer although it will not be quite as thick.

FRENCH ONION SOUP

*This soup tastes best if cooked the day
before it is needed and then reheated as required.*

SERVES 4

3 medium onions
4 tbsps butter or margarine
2 tbsps all-purpose flour or soya flour
4⅓ cups boiling vegetable stock or
    water plus 2 bouillon cubes
Salt and pepper

Topping
4 slices French bread, cut crosswise
½ cup cheddar cheese, grated
¼ cup Parmesan cheese, grated

1. Slice the onions very finely into rings.

2. Melt the butter in a pan, add the onion rings and fry over a medium heat until well browned.

3. Mix in the flour and stir well until browned.

4. Add the stock and seasoning and simmer for 30 minutes.

5. Toast the bread on both sides.

6. Combine the cheese, and divide between the bread slices; broil until golden brown.

7. Place the slices of bread and cheese in the bottom of individual soup dishes and spoon the soup over the top.

8. Serve at once.

TIME: Preparation takes 10 minutes, cooking takes 30 minutes.

VARIATION: For a special occasion, add a tablespoonful of brandy to the stock.

WATCHPOINT: The onions must be very well browned, as this gives the rich color to the soup.

Gazpacho

One of Spain's tastiest exports.

SERVES 4

1lb ripe tomatoes
1 small onion
1 small green pepper
1 clove garlic, crushed
¼ medium cucumber
1 tbsp red wine vinegar
1 tbsp olive oil
14oz can tomato juice
1-2 tbsps lime juice
Salt and pepper

1. Plunge the tomatoes into boiling water, leave for 2 minutes, then remove the skins and seeds.

2. Chop the onion and pepper and place in a food processor with the tomatoes, garlic, cucumber, vinegar, oil and tomato juice.

3. Purée until smooth.

4. Add the lime juice and seasoning to taste.

5. Pour the soup into a glass dish and chill until required.

TIME: Preparation takes 10 minutes.

SERVING IDEA: Serve garnished with croutons and finely diced cucumber.

WATCHPOINT: If the soup is too thick, add more tomato juice after Step 5.

VARIATION: Lemon juice may be used in place of the lime juice.

SWEET POTATO SOUP

Warm up your winter nights with this heartening soup.

SERVES 4-6

4 tbsps butter or margarine
1 large onion, finely chopped
1lb sweet potatoes, peeled and diced
1¼ cups carrots, peeled and diced
1 tbsp chopped coriander (cilantro)
1 lemon, zest and juice
3¾ cups stock
Pepper

1. Melt the butter or margarine and cook the onion until transparent.

2. Add the sweet potatoes and carrots and allow to "sweat" over a very low heat for 10-15 minutes, stirring occasionally.

3. Add the coriander, lemon zest, juice of half the lemon, stock and pepper.

4. Cover and simmer for 30-40 minutes.

5. Process until almost smooth, but leaving some texture to the soup.

6. Return to the pan and reheat until piping hot.

7. Garnish with coriander leaves and serve immediately.

TIME: Preparation takes 15 minutes, cooking takes 40-55 minutes.

SERVING IDEA: Serve with whole-grain rolls.

COOK'S TIP: Fresh coriander or cilantro may be kept in a pitcher of water in a cool place. It can also be frozen to use when fresh is not available.

Cee Jay Ratatouille

The ratatouille can be made in advance and reheated before covering with the apples.

SERVES 6

1 medium onion, finely sliced
3 cloves garlic, crushed
4 tbsps olive oil
1 large eggplant, diced
1 large red pepper, sliced
2 medium zucchini, sliced
4 medium tomatoes, sliced
1 tsp oregano
Salt and pepper
2 large apples, peeled and thinly sliced
2 tbsps butter or margarine
Ground cloves

1. Sauté the onion and garlic in the oil until the onion is transparent.

2. Add the eggplant, pepper, zucchini and tomatoes.

3. Cook for a further 5 minutes, stirring occasionally.

4. Add the oregano and seasoning and simmer, covered, for 15-20 minutes.

5. Divide the ratatouille between 6 heated ovenproof dishes and arrange a layer of finely sliced apple on top.

6. Melt the butter or margarine and brush over the top of the apples.

7. Sprinkle with a good pinch of ground cloves and broil until the apples are brown and puffy.

8. Serve immediately.

TIME: Preparation takes 15 minutes, cooking takes 30 minutes.

COOK'S TIP: This dish will happily keep in a moderate oven for up to 30 minutes.

PAMPLEMOUSSE

The French word for grapefruit gives this light and easy appetizer its name.

SERVES 6

3 large grapefruit
3 red skinned apples
4 sticks celery
24 grapes (red or green)
4 tbsps heavy cream

1. Halve the grapefruit crosswise and cut around the inside of the skin to loosen the flesh.

2. Make deep cuts between the segments, close to the membranes, and remove the segments making sure you do not pierce the skins.

3. Put into a large bowl with any of the juice.

4. Cut away any remaining membranes from the shells with a pair of kitchen scissors, put the grapefruit shells into a plastic bag and store in the refrigerator.

5. Remove the cores from the well washed apples and dice but do not peel.

6. Chop the celery finely.

7. Halve the grapes and remove any seeds.

8. Add the apples, celery and grapes to the grapefruit and stir in the cream.

9. Refrigerate until required.

10. Just before serving, stir well and pile the mixture into the grapefruit skins.

11. Serve at once.

TIME: Preparation takes 10 minutes.

SERVING IDEA: To make "Vandyke" grapefruit, snip small V-shapes from the edges of the empty half shells with scissors. Serve garnished with fresh mint leaves, if desired.

WATERCRESS AND MUSHROOM PÂTÉ

*A delightful pâté which is perfect garnished with lime
or lemon wedges and served with thinly
sliced brown bread and butter.*

SERVES 4

4 tbsps butter
1 medium onion, finely chopped
3oz large mushrooms, finely chopped
1 bunch watercress, finely chopped
1 cup low fat cream cheese
Few drops shoyu sauce (Japanese soy
    sauce)
Scant ½ tsp caraway seeds
Black pepper

1. Melt the butter over a low heat and cook the onion until soft but not colored.

2. Raise the heat, add the mushrooms and cook quickly for 2 minutes.

3. Put in the chopped watercress and stir for about 30 seconds until it becomes limp.

4. Place the contents of the pan in a blender or food processor together with the cheese and shoyu sauce.

5. Blend until smooth.

6. Stir in the caraway seeds and pepper to taste.

7. Put into individual ramekin dishes or one large serving dish and chill for at least 2 hours until firm.

TIME: Preparation takes 10 minutes, cooking takes 5 minutes.

COOK'S TIP: It may be necessary to stir the ingredients several times while processing as the mixture will be fairly thick.

CRUDITÉS

A great favorite served with delicious dips to accompany.

SERVES 6-8

Choose from the following vegetable selection:

Cauliflower, broccoli - divided into small florets

Carrots, celery, zucchini, cucumber – cut into matchstick pieces

Chicory – separate the blades

Mushrooms – sliced or quartered

Peppers, kohlrabi, fennel – sliced

Radishes, green onions, cherry tomatoes – leave whole

Tomato and Cheese Dip

1 tbsp butter or margarine
1 tbsp grated onion
8oz tomatoes, peeled and diced
½ cup cheddar cheese, grated
½ cup fresh breadcrumbs
1 egg, beaten
½ tsp dried mustard
Salt and pepper
2-4 tbsps thick set plain yogurt

Creamed Curry Dip

1 tbsp mango chutney
6 tbsps home-made or good quality mayonnaise
1 tsp curry paste
2 tbsps heavy cream
Pinch ground cumin

Avocado Dip

2 ripe avocados
1 onion, diced
½ clove garlic, crushed
2 tbsps lemon juice
Salt and pepper

Tomato and Cheese Dip

1. Melt the butter or margarine and gently fry the onion for 2 or 3 minutes until soft.

2. Add the tomatoes, cover and simmer for 10 minutes.

3. Add the cheese, breadcrumbs and egg and cook for a further minute, stirring all the time, until thickened. Do not allow to boil.

4. Add the mustard and seasoning and blend or process until smooth.

5. Mix in enough yogurt to ensure a smooth "dipping" consistency and store in the refrigerator until required.

Creamed Curry Dip

1. Chop the pieces of mango with a sharp knife and place in a bowl.

2. Add the other ingredients and mix well.

3. Refrigerate until required.

Avocado Dip

1. Peel the avocados, remove the stones and chop the flesh roughly.

2. Process or blend together with the onion, garlic and lemon juice until smooth.

3. Season to taste and refrigerate until required.

TIME: Preparation takes 30 minutes, cooking takes 15 minutes.

FLAGEOLET FIESTA

*Serve this dish on its own as an appetizer or as
a snack with lots of crusty bread.*

SERVES 4

1 cup flageolet beans, soaked overnight
1 medium onion
1 clove garlic
Half a cucumber
2 tbsps chopped parsley
2 tbsps chopped mint
2 tbsps olive oil
Juice and grated rind of 1 lemon
Salt
Freshly ground black pepper
Watercress to garnish

1. Cook the flageolet beans in plenty of boiling water for about 1 hour or until just tender.

2. Drain and put into a mixing bowl.

3. Peel and finely chop the onion.

4. Crush the garlic and chop the cucumber into bite-sized pieces.

5. Add the onion, garlic, cucumber, herbs, oil, lemon juice and rind to the beans and mix well.

6. Add seasoning to taste and leave to marinate for 2 hours.

7. Transfer to a clean serving bowl.

8. Serve garnished with watercress.

TIME: Preparation takes 15 minutes. Marinating takes 2 hours and cooking takes 1 hour.

VARIATION: Substitute red kidney beans or black-eyed beans for the flageolet beans.

PARSNIP FRITTERS

These tasty fritters make a nice change for lunch or a light snack.

SERVES 4

1 cup all-purpose flour
2 tsps baking powder
1 tsp salt
½ tsp pepper
1 egg
⅔ cup milk
1 tbsp melted butter
3-4 cooked parsnips, finely diced
Oil or clarified butter for frying.

1. Mix together the flour, baking powder, salt and pepper.

2. Beat the egg and mix with the milk and melted butter.

3. Stir this mixture into the dry ingredients.

4. Stir in the cooked parsnips.

5. Divide the mixture into 16 and shape into small fritters.

6. Fry in oil or clarified butter until browned on both sides.

TIME: Preparation takes 10 minutes, cooking takes about 5-8 minutes per batch.

VARIATION: Zucchini, corn, onions or eggplant may be substituted for the parsnips.

SERVING IDEA: Serve with yogurt sauce or make them slightly larger and serve as a main course with salad.

RED LENTIL SOUFFLÉ

Serve this tasty soufflé as an appetizer or with watercress or salad for a light lunch.

SERVES 4

½ cup red lentils
1 bay leaf
1¼ cups water
2 tbsps margarine or butter
⅓ cup heavy cream
2 egg yolks
3 egg whites
½ cup grated cheddar cheese (optional)
Salt and pepper
Pinch of paprika

1. Pick over the lentils and remove any grit. Rinse well.

2. Place the lentils, bay leaf and water in a pan and bring to the boil.

3. Simmer for 20 minutes or until the lentils are soft.

4. Remove the bay leaf and beat the lentils until they are very smooth.

5. Beat in the margarine, cream and egg yolks.

6. Beat the egg whites until very stiff and fold into the mixture.

7. Season and fold in the grated cheese.

8. Pour into a well greased soufflé dish and sprinkle with a little paprika.

9. Bake in a preheated oven 375°F for approximately 20 minutes or until the soufflé is well risen, firm and brown.

10. Serve immediately.

TIME: Preparation takes about 15 minutes, cooking takes 40 minutes.

VARIATION: Add a good pinch of mixed herbs to the lentils while cooking.

MIXED NUT BALLS

*This versatile dish can be made in advance and
refrigerated until required for cooking.*
SERVES 8

⅔ cup ground almonds
⅔ cup ground hazelnuts
⅔ cup ground pecan nuts
¾ cup whole-wheat breadcrumbs
1 cup cheddar cheese, grated
1 egg, beaten
4-5 tbsps dry sherry or 2 tbsps milk and 3
   tbsps dry sherry
1 small onion, finely chopped
1 tbsp grated fresh ginger
1 tbsp fresh parsley, chopped
1 small red or green chili pepper,
   finely chopped
1 medium red pepper, diced
1 tsp sea salt
1 tsp freshly ground black pepper

1. Mix the almonds, hazelnuts and pecan
nuts together with the breadcrumbs and
the cheese.

2. In another bowl, mix the beaten egg
with the sherry, onion, ginger, parsley,
chili and red pepper.

3. Combine with the nut mixture and add
the salt and pepper.

4. If the mixture is too dry, add a little
more sherry or milk.

5. Form into small 1-inch balls.

6. Do not preheat the oven.

7. Arrange the balls on a well greased
baking sheet and bake at 180°C for about
20-25 minutes, until golden brown.

TIME: Preparation takes about 20 minutes, cooking takes 20-25 minutes.

SERVING IDEA: Serve on individual plates on a bed of chopped lettuce. Garnish with slices
of lemon and pass your favorite sauce in a separate bowl.

HUMMUS

A classic first course which also makes the perfect snack.

SERVES 4

1 cup cooked chick peas or garbanzo
   beans (reserve liquid)
4 tbsps light tahini (sesame paste)
Juice of 2 lemons
6 tbsps olive oil
3-4 cloves garlic, crushed
Salt to taste

1. Put the cooked chick peas into a food processor together with ⅔ cup of the reserved liquid.

2. Add the tahini, lemon juice, half of the olive oil, the garlic, and salt.

3. Blend until smooth, adding a little more liquid if it is too thick.

4. Leave to stand for an hour or so to let the flavors develop.

5. Serve on individual dishes with the remaining olive oil drizzled over the top.

TIME: Preparation takes 10 minutes, standing time takes 1 hour.

SERVING IDEA: Serve sprinkled with paprika and garnished with wedges of lemon. Accompany the hummus with warm pitta bread.

VARIATION: Canned chick peas or garbanzo beans can be used. Substitute can liquid for cooking liquid.

BULGAR BOATS

This pretty dish can easily be taken on picnics.

SERVES 6

¼ cup green lentils
½ cup bulgar
1 red pepper
1 green pepper
1 medium onion
½ cup pine nuts (dry roasted in a pan)
2 tsps chopped herbs (tarragon, chives or parsley)
Juice and rind of l lemon
Salt
Freshly ground black pepper
Romaine lettuce to serve

---

1. Remove any grit or stones from the lentils and rinse well.

2. Cover with plenty of water and boil for about 20 minutes - do not overcook.

3. Place the bulgar wheat in a mixing bowl and cover with boiling water. Leave for about 10 minutes - the grain will then have swollen, softened and absorbed the water.

4. Dice the peppers and chop the onion finely.

5. Drain the lentils and add to the wheat, together with the peppers, nuts, onion, herbs, lemon juice and rind, salt and pepper.

6. Using one large lettuce leaf per person, spoon the salad into the center of the leaves and arrange on a large serving dish garnished with wedges of lemon.

TIME: Preparation takes 15 minutes, cooking takes 20 minutes.

VARIATION: Cashews or peanuts could be used instead of pine nuts. The bulgar mixture could be served in 'parcels' of lightly blanched cabbage leaves.

COOK'S TIP: If the salad is not required immediately, cover and refrigerate until needed.

FENNEL AND ORANGE CROUSTADE

A delicious mixture which is simple to prepare.

SERVES 4

4 x 1-inch thick slices whole-wheat bread
Oil for deep frying
2 fennel bulbs (reserve any fronds)
4 oranges
1 tbsp olive oil
Pinch salt
Chopped fresh mint for garnishing

1. Trim the crust off the bread and cut into 3-inch squares.

2. Hollow out the middles, leaving evenly shaped cases.

3. Heat the oil and deep-fry the bread until golden brown.

4. Drain the bread well on absorbent kitchen paper. Leave to cool.

5. Trim the fennel bulbs and slice thinly. Place in a mixing bowl.

6. Remove all the peel and pith from the oranges and cut into segments - do this over the mixing bowl to catch the juice.

7. Mix the orange segments with the fennel.

8. Add the olive oil and salt and mix together thoroughly.

9. Just before serving, divide the fennel and orange mixture evenly between the bread cases and garnish with fresh mint and fennel fronds.

TIME: Preparation takes 15 minutes, cooking takes 5 minutes.

VARIATION: Serve the salad with the croustades. Sprinkle with croutons instead.

COOK'S TIP: The salad can be made in advance and refrigerated until required but do not fill the cases until just before serving.

CARROT AND CORN MEDLEY

*A delicious combination which is perfect as a
light appetizer or summer snack.*

SERVES 6

---

llb carrots
1 clove garlic, crushed
2-3 tbsps lemon juice
Salt
Freshly ground black pepper
12oz can corn
Lettuce
½ inch piece of fresh root ginger, grated
Few black olives, stones removed

---

1. Scrub and grate the carrots and place in a mixing bowl.

2. Combine the garlic, lemon juice, salt and pepper in a screw topped jar and shake well.

3. Mix the dressing with the grated carrot and add the sweetcorn.

4. Put a little finely shredded lettuce in the bottom of individual stem glasses and arrange the carrot and corn mixture on the top.

5. Garnish with grated ginger and olives.

6. Chill for 30 minutes before serving.

TIME: Preparation takes 15 minutes, chilling takes 30 minutes.

SERVING IDEA: Serve with whole-wheat bread and butter triangles.

VARIATION: To use as an accompaniment to a main course – arrange the carrot on a wide serving plate, leaving an indentation in the center. Fill this with the corn and garnish with ginger and olives.

DATE, APPLE AND CELERY APPETIZER

A healthy dish with a tasty mix of flavors.

SERVES 4

4 tsps finely grated coconut
2 crisp eating apples
3-4 sticks celery
¾ cup dates
2 tbsps plain yogurt
Salt and pepper
Pinch of nutmeg

1. Toast the coconut in a dry frying pan over a low heat until it is golden brown, then put to one side.

2. Core and dice the apples and chop the celery finely.

3. Plunge the dates into boiling water, drain and chop finely.

4. Combine the apples, celery and dates in a mixing bowl.

5. Add the yogurt, seasoning and nutmeg and mix thoroughly so that the salad is coated completely.

6. Transfer to a serving bowl and garnish with the toasted coconut.

7. Serve at once.

TIME: Preparation takes 10 minutes, cooking takes 2-3 minutes.

SERVING IDEA: Serve individual portions on a bed of watercress.

COOK'S TIP: Red skinned apples add color to this salad.

Mushrooms and Tofu in Garlic Butter

A quick and delicious first course.

SERVES 4

3 cups small mushrooms
1 inch piece root ginger
8oz smoked tofu (bean curd)
1 stick butter
4 small cloves garlic, crushed
2 tbsps chopped parsley

1. Wipe the mushrooms with a damp cloth.

2. Peel and grate the root ringer.

3. Cut the smoked tofu into small ½-inch squares.

4. Melt the butter in a frying pan.

5. Add the crushed garlic and ginger and fry gently for two minutes.

6. Add the mushrooms and cook gently for 4-5 minutes until the mushrooms are softened.

7. Finally, add the smoked tofu and heat through.

8. Divide between 4 individually heated dishes, sprinkle with chopped parsley and serve at once.

TIME: Preparation takes 10 minutes, cooking takes 12 minutes.

SERVING IDEA: Serve with French bread or crusty wholemeal rolls.

VARIATION: Substitute asparagus tips for the mushrooms. Plain tofu which has been drained overnight can be used if the smoked variety is unavailable.

SAVORY TOMATOES

An ideal appetizer for dieters.

SERVES 4

4 large beefsteak tomatoes
4 tbsps cottage cheese
1 tsp ground cumin
1 green pepper, de-seeded and diced
Salt and pepper
¼ cup pumpkin seeds
1 bunch watercress

1. Slice off the tops of the tomatoes.

2. Remove the seeds and leave upside down to drain.

3. Rub the cottage cheese through a strainer to achieve a smooth consistency, add a little milk if necessary.

4. Stir in the cumin, pepper and seasoning.

5. Divide the mixture into four and stuff the tomatoes.

6. Dry roast the pumpkin seeds in a frying pan until they are lightly browned. Sprinkle over the tomatoes.

7. Chill until required.

8. Serve on a bed of watercress.

TIME: Preparation takes 10 minutes.

SERVING IDEA: Serve with very thin slices of brown bread and butter.

VARIATION: Use cream cheese in place of the cottage cheese.

Dhingri Kari (Mushroom Curry)

An ideal snack or supper dish.

SERVES 4

1½ cups leeks, finely sliced
2 cloves garlic, crushed
½ tsp grated ginger
2 tsps curry powder
1 tsp garam masala
2 tbsps oil
6 cups mushrooms, cut into quarters
½ cup coconut, grated
1 cup water
1 tbsp lemon juice

1. Fry the leeks, garlic, ginger and spices in the oil until soft.

2. Add the mushrooms and cook over a low heat until soft.

3. Add the grated coconut and half of the water. Cook gently until the coconut has completely softened, adding extra water if the mixture appears too dry.

4. Stir in the lemon juice and sufficient salt to taste.

5. Serve on a bed of rice.

TIME: Preparation takes 15 minutes, cooking takes about 20 minutes.

SERVING IDEA: Serve with a tomato and onion salad.

POTATO NESTS

*An ideal supper dish and an excellent
way of using up leftover cooked potatoes.*

SERVES 2

1 onion, finely chopped
3 medium potatoes, cooked in their skins
A little milk
1 tbsp butter
Salt and pepper
2 eggs
¼ cup cheese, grated

1. Cook the onion in a little water until softened. Drain.

2. Peel the cooked potatoes and mash them with the milk, butter and seasoning.

3. Add the drained onion and mix well.

4. Divide the mixture into two and make "nests" on a greased baking sheet.

5. Crack an egg into each nest and sprinkle with grated cheese.

6. Bake at 400°F for 20-25 minutes or until the eggs are set.

TIME: Preparation takes 10 minutes, cooking takes 25-30 minutes.

SERVING IDEA: Garnish with parsley and serve with beans and broiled tomatoes or a salad.

VARIATION: The nests may be filled with chopped leftover nut roast mixed with a mushroom or tomato sauce and a few freshly chopped herbs.

POLYGARDOO

*An adaptable bean dish which can be served
as a snack, side dish or main meal.*

SERVES 4

1 onion, finely chopped
1 clove garlic, crushed
1 tsp bouillon powder dissolved in a little
   boiling water
1½ cups mushrooms, wiped and sliced
1 small green pepper, chopped
14oz can tomatoes, drained
1 pinch of any herb – oregano, sage,
   thyme or mixed herbs
14oz can navy beans
Salt and pepper
1 tbsp lemon juice
2 tbsps plain yogurt

1. Cook the onion and garlic with the bouillon powder and water until softened a little.

2. Add the mushrooms and chopped pepper and continue cooking for 3-4 minutes.

3. Add the tomatoes, herbs, beans and seasoning.

4. Mix well and simmer gently for 5 minutes.

5. Remove from the heat and stir in the lemon juice and yogurt.

TIME: Preparation takes 10 minutes, cooking takes 15 minutes.

SERVING IDEA: Serve with pitta bread, rice or pasta for a main meal.

VARIATION: Any type of cooked beans may be used in this dish.

FILO TWISTS

Serve these delicious snacks anywhere –
buffets, picnics, or drinks parties.

SERVES 4

½ cup dried mixed fruit
¼ cup figs, chopped
½ cup ground almonds
½ cup dates, chopped
½ cup walnuts, chopped
1 tbsp brown sugar
½ tsp ground cinnamon
Zest and juice of 1 orange
2 tbsps melted butter plus 1 tbsp
   melted butter
16 sheets filo or strudel pastry,
   approximately 1 inch x 8 inch square

1. Put the mixed fruit, figs, ground almonds, dates and walnuts into a mixing bowl.

2. Add the sugar, cinnamon, zest and juice of the orange and the 2 tbsps melted butter. Mix together well and set aside.

3. Use two sheets together for each twist. Divide the mixture into 8 and place one portion of the filling in the center of each sheet.

4. Fold the base of the filo over the filling and roll up.

5. Twist the ends of the filo roll where there is no filling, to form the shape.

6. Place on a greased baking sheet and brush generously with the remaining melted butter.

7. Cook at 400°F for 20 minutes or until golden brown and crisp.

TIME: Preparation takes 20 minutes, cooking takes 20 minutes.

SERVING IDEA: Serve with orange wedges.

COOK'S TIP: Frozen filo or strudel pastry may be purchased at most large supermarkets. Allow 2 hours to defrost at room temperature or 3 minutes in a microwave.

WATCHPOINT: A little extra care must be taken when handling this pastry and it must always be kept well wrapped before use to avoid drying out.

IMAM BAYILDI

Imam Bayildi means "the priest has fainted".
Apparently the dish was so delicious that the
priest fainted with delight!

SERVES 4

---

2 large eggplants
Salt
⅔ cup olive oil
2 onions, peeled and finely chopped
2 cloves garlic, crushed
2 cups tomatoes, skinned and chopped
½ tsp allspice
Juice of ½ lemon
1 tsp brown sugar
1 tbsp chopped parsley
1 tbsp pine kernels
Salt and pepper

---

1. Halve the eggplants lengthwise, and scoop out the flesh with a sharp knife leaving a substantial shell so they do not disintegrate when cooked.

2. Sprinkle the shells with a little salt and leave upside down on a plate for 30 minutes to drain away any bitter juices.

3. Meanwhile, heat half the oil in a saucepan and fry the onion and garlic until just softened.

4. Add the scooped out eggplant flesh, tomatoes, allspice, lemon juice, sugar, parsley, pine kernels and a little seasoning.

5. Simmer for about 20 minutes until the mixture has thickened.

6. Wash and dry the eggplant shells and spoon the filling into the halves.

7. Place side by side in a buttered ovenproof dish.

8. Mix the remaining oil with ⅔ cup water and a little seasoning.

9. Pour around the eggplants and bake at 350°F for 30-40 minutes or until completely tender.

TIME: Preparation takes 25 minutes, cooking takes 1 hour.

SERVING IDEA: Serve hot or cold garnished with fresh herbs and accompanied by chunks of whole-wheat bread. If serving cold, chill for at least 2 hours before serving.

CAULIFLOWER AND BROCCOLI SOUFFLETTES

Serve as a winter-time first course or as a main meal with rice salad and ratatouille.

SERVES 6

12oz cauliflower
12oz broccoli
4 tbsps margarine
½ cup whole-wheat or brown rice flour
Scant 2 cups milk
½ cup cheddar cheese, grated
1 large egg, separated
Good pinch of nutmeg

1. Break the cauliflower and broccoli into small foorets and steam until just tender – about 7-10 minutes.

2. Melt the margarine, remove from the heat and gradually add the flour. Stir to a roux and add the milk gradually, blending well to ensure a smooth consistency.

3. Return the pan to the heat and stir until the sauce thickens and comes to the boil.

4. Cool a little and add the egg yolk and cheese, stir well and add nutmeg to taste.

5. Whip the egg white until stiff and fold carefully into the sauce.

6. Place the vegetables into 6 small buttered ramekin dishes and season.

7. Divide the sauce evenly between the dishes and bake immediately at 375°F for about 35 minutes until puffed and golden.

8. Serve at once.

TIME: Preparation takes 15 minutes, cooking takes 50 minutes.

SALADS FOR ALL SEASONS

"To remember a good salad is generally to remember a successful dinner; at all events, the dinner necessarily includes the perfect salad."

George Ellwanger
Pleasures of the Table 1903

Raw vegetables have always been an important part of our diet and for optimum health it is important that raw food in some form be eaten every day. We are lucky nowadays to find a wide variety of salad ingredients available all year round, although they do tend to be expensive out of season. Today the choice of produce is endless and with organically grown produce you can be sure that the vegetables have not be treated with chemical sprays or pesticides. Nearly all vegetables are suitable for use in salads, and eaten this way they provide more nutrients than cooked vegetables, as even with careful cooking, valuable vitamins and minerals are lost.

Vegetables are a valuable source of fiber, vitamins and minerals and although in most cases they are 80 per cent water, the other 20 per cent contains carbohydrates, fat and protein. To many people, a salad is just a random mix of lettuce, cucumber and tomato. A good salad, however, should be pleasing to the eye as well as the palate. It can be as vibrant as you wish, using red, green and orange peppers, tomatoes, green onions, carrots and lettuce, or it can be a mix of greens using lettuce, cabbage, cucumber, avocado, green onions and green peppers. The list of ingredients that can be used in salads is as long as your own imagination, so experiment and you will find a salad for every season and every occasion.

GREEK SALAD

A great favorite which has the added
advantage of being easy to prepare.

SERVES 4

2 tomatoes
½ green pepper
¼ cucumber
2 sticks celery, finely sliced
1 tsp fresh basil, finely chopped
Few crisp leaves of lettuce
1 cup Feta cheese, diced
16 black olives, pitted

Dressing
4 tbsps olive oil
2 tbsps lemon juice
1 clove garlic, crushed
Large pinch oregano
Salt and pepper

1. Cut each tomato into eight pieces and put into a large mixing bowl.

2. Chop the pepper and cucumber roughly. Add to the tomato together with the celery and chopped basil.

3. Mix together the oil, lemon juice, garlic, oregano and seasoning, and pour over the salad.

4. Mix well to coat all the vegetables.

5. Arrange a few leaves of lettuce in the bottom of a serving bowl, and pile the salad on the top, followed by the cheese cubes.

6. Garnish with olives.

TIME: Preparation takes 15 minutes.

SERVING IDEA: Serve with pitta bread.

VARIATION: Add a few croutons just before serving.

TABOULEH

*This is a traditional salad from the Middle East. The main
ingredient is bulgar which is partially cooked cracked wheat and
only needs soaking for a short while before it is ready to eat.*

SERVES 6

¾ cup bulgar wheat
1 tsp salt
1½ cups boiling water
1lb tomatoes, chopped
½ cucumber, diced
3-4 green onions

Dressing
¼ cup olive oil
¼ cup lemon juice
2 tbsps fresh mint
4 tbsps fresh parsley
2 cloves garlic, crushed

1. Mix the bulgar wheat with the salt,
pour over the boiling water and leave for
15-20 minutes. All the water will then be
absorbed.

2. Mix together the ingredients for the
dressing and pour over the soaked bulgar.

3. Fold in lightly with a spoon.

4. Leave for two hours or overnight in a
fridge or cool place.

5. Add the salad ingredients and serve.

TIME: Preparation takes about 20 minutes, standing time is about 2 hours.

COOK'S TIP: A few cooked beans can be added to make this dish more substantial.

SERVING IDEA: Serve with pizzas, quiches and roasts.

Wheatberry Salad

*This makes a substantial salad dish which provides an
almost perfect protein balance.*

SERVES 4

---

1 cup wheatberries, cooked
½ cup kidney beans, cooked
3 medium tomatoes
4 green onions, chopped
2 sticks celery, chopped
1 tbsp pumpkin seeds

Dressing
4 tbsps olive or sunflower oil
2 tbsps red wine vinegar
1 clove garlic, crushed
1 tsp grated fresh ginger
1 tsp paprika
1 tbsp shoyu (Japanese soy sauce)
Fresh or dried oregano, to taste
Ground black pepper

1. Mix the salad ingredients together, reserving a few pumpkin seeds and green onions for garnishing.

2. Shake the dressing ingredients together in a screw-topped jar.

3. Pour over the salad and mix gently.

TIME: Preparation takes 20 minutes.

SERVING IDEA: Serve with a lettuce salad.
Wheatberries also mix well with grated carrot and an orange dressing.

COOK'S TIP: This salad keeps well so it can be made in advance and kept in the refrigerator until required.

MUSHROOM WALDORF SALAD

Decorate the top of this salad with a line of sliced strawberries or kiwi fruit.

SERVES 4

3 large mushrooms, thinly sliced
1 medium apple, cut into chunks and
    coated with lemon juice
2 celery sticks, cut into matchsticks
¼ cup walnut pieces
1 bunch watercress

Dressing
1 tbsp mayonnaise
1 tbsp thick yogurt
½ tsp herb-flavored mustard
A little lemon juice
Salt and pepper

1. Place the mushrooms, apple, celery and walnuts in a bowl.

2. Combine all the ingredients for the dressing and mix gently with the vegetables.

3. Arrange the watercress on a flat dish or platter and mound the salad mixture on the top.

TIME: Preparation takes about 10 minutes.

VARIATION: A medium bulb of fennel, finely sliced, could be used in place of the celery.

PASTA AND AVOCADO SALAD

The perfect lunch or supper salad for guests.

SERVES 4

---

2 cups pasta shapes
3 tbsps mayonnaise
2 tsps tahini (sesame paste)
1 orange
½ medium red pepper, chopped
1 medium avocado
Pumpkin seeds to garnish

---

1. Cook the pasta until tender and leave to cool.

2. Mix together the mayonnaise and tahini.

3. Segment the orange and chop into small pieces, retaining any juice.

4. Chop the pepper.

5. Stir the mayonnaise mixture, pepper and orange (plus juice) into the pasta.

6. Just before serving, cube the avocado and stir in carefully.

7. Serve on an oval dish, decorated with pumpkin seeds.

TIME: Preparation takes 10 minutes, cooking takes about 35 minutes.

WATCHPOINT: Do not peel the avocado until required as it may discolor.

VARIATION: Green pepper may be used in place of the red pepper.

CUCUMBER SALAD

Finely chopped celery may be used in place of fennel in this recipe.

SERVES 6

1 whole cucumber
1 red apple
1 medium-sized fennel, reserve feathery
   leaves for decoration
1 tbsp pine nuts

Dressing
3 tbsps corn oil or sunflower oil
2 tbsps cider vinegar
2 tbsps fresh dill or 1 tsp dried dill
1 tsp caraway seeds
1-2 tsps paprika
Salt and pepper to taste

1. Wash the cucumber but do not peel. Cut it very thinly and place the slices in a strainer. Leave to drain for about 20 minutes.

2. Wash and core the apple, slice thinly.

3. Wash and trim the fennel, removing the tough outer leaves and stem. Slice finely.

4. Combine all the ingredients for the dressing and mix well.

5. Mix with the drained cucumber slices, apple, fennel and pine nuts.

6. Place the salad in the refrigerator or keep in a cool place for about an hour before serving.

TIME: Preparation takes 30 minutes.

SERVING IDEA: Serve decorated with finely chopped fennel leaves.

LOLLO ROSSO SALAD

A colorful variation of a Greek Salad.

SERVES 4

½ Lollo Rosso lettuce
3 medium tomatoes, diced
1 red pepper, chopped
1 green pepper, chopped
3 sticks celery, diced
⅓ cucumber, diced
4 cups cheddar cheese
16 black olives, pitted

Dressing
1 tbsp tarragon vinegar
3 tbsps olive oil

1. Wash the lettuce and dry it well. Break into pieces with your fingers and put it into a large bowl.

2. Add the tomatoes, pepper, celery, cucumber and cheese.

3. Mix together the vinegar and olive oil, and pour over the salad.

4. Mix gently.

5. Divide the salad between 4 individual dishes and place 4 olives on the top of each one.

TIME: Preparation takes about 10 minutes.

SERVING IDEA: Serve for lunch with crusty rolls or French bread.

VARIATION: If you do not like olives, substitute havled, de-seeded purple grapes. Any crisp lettuce leaves can be used.

COOK'S TIP: To keep celery crisp, wash well and place the sticks in a cold water in the refrigerator.

RADISH SALAD

Serve this simple salad with a quiche or pizza for a light luncheon dish.

SERVES 4

3 bunches radishes
1 medium onion
2 large tomatoes
2 tbsps olive oil
2 tbsps lemon juice
Salt and pepper
1 tbsp chopped parsley

1. Slice the radishes and onion finely.

2. Peel and slice the tomatoes.

3. Arrange the vegetables on a serving dish.

4. Put the oil, lemon juice and seasoning into a screw topped jar and shake well.

5. Pour the dressing over the vegetables.

6. Sprinkle with the chopped parsley.

7. Chill before serving.

TIME: Preparation takes 15 minutes. Chilling takes about 30 minutes.

VARIATION: Use red wine vinegar instead of the lemon juice.
Daikon radish (white radish) can be used in place of the red radishes.

MARINATED CARROT SALAD

The perfect light lunch dish or accompaniment to burgers or roasts.

SERVES 4-5

1lb carrots
1 medium onion
1 medium green pepper

Dressing
½ cup tomato juice
½ cup olive oil
½ cup cider vinegar
2 tsps brown sugar
1 level tsp dry mustard power
Salt and pepper

1. Peel the carrots and cut into matchsticks.

2. Cover with water, bring to the boil and simmer for 4-5 minutes. Drain and allow to cool a little.

3. Slice the onion finely into rings.

4. Cut the pepper into strips.

5. Mix together the dressing ingredients until well blended.

6. Combine the carrots with the onion and pepper and pour the dressing over the top.

7. Marinate overnight, stirring occasionally.

8. Serve garnished with chopped parsley and lemon slices.

TIME: Preparation takes 10 minutes, cooking takes 5 minutes. Marinate overnight.

SERVING IDEA: Serve with cubed cheese and bread to mop up the juices.

BAVARIAN POTATO SALAD

It is best to prepare this salad a few hours in advance to allow the potatoes to absorb the flavors.

SERVES 4-6

2lbs tiny new potatoes
4 tbsps olive oil
4 green onions, finely chopped
1 clove garlic, crushed
2 tbsps fresh dill, chopped or 1 tbsp dried
2 tbsps wine vinegar
½ tsp sugar
Salt and pepper
2 tbsps chopped fresh parsley

1. Wash the potatoes but do not peel, put them into a pan, cover with water and boil until just tender.

2. Whilst the potatoes are cooking, heat the olive oil in a frying pan and cook the green onions and garlic for 2-3 minutes until they have softened a little.

3. Add the dill and cook gently for a further minute.

4. Add the wine vinegar and sugar, and stir until the sugar dissolves. Remove from the heat and add a little seasoning.

5. Drain the potatoes and pour the dressing over them while they are still hot.

6. Allow to cool and sprinkle with the chopped parsley before serving.

TIME: Preparation takes 15 minutes, cooking takes 15 minutes.

CUCUMBER AND PINEAPPLE SALAD

*If you do not have fresh pineapple, use canned
pineapple without added sugar.*

SERVES 4

4 tsps raisins
2 tbsps pineapple juice
½ cucumber
1 red pepper
2 cups pineapple chunks
3 tbsps oil and vinegar dressing
1 tsp fresh mint, finely chopped
2 tsps sesame seeds

1. Soak the raisins in the pineapple juice for at least half an hour.

2. Slice the cucumber finely.

3. Cut the pepper in half, de-seed, remove the core and chop finely.

4. If using fresh pineapple, chop into cubes.

5. Arrange the cucumber on a serving dish.

6. Mix the pepper, pineapple and raisins together and pile in the center of the cucumber.

7. Mix the mint into the dressing and pour over the salad just before serving.

8. Sprinkle the sesame seeds over the top.

TIME: Preparation takes 10 minutes, soaking takes 30 minutes.

SPINACH SALAD

Serve with a simple main course.

SERVES 4-6

1lb spinach
1 medium red cabbage
1 medium onion
1 cup apricots
6 tbsps oil and vinegar dressing
½ cup toasted sunflower seeds

---

1. Wash the spinach and drain well.

2. First remove the outer leaves and core, then slice the cabbage finely.

3. Slice the onion finely and cut the apricots into slivers.

4. Tear the spinach leaves into bite-sized pieces and put into a serving dish.

5. Add the sliced cabbage, onion and apricots.

6. Pour over the dressing and mix together thoroughly.

7. Sprinkle with sunflower seeds and serve.

TIME: Preparation takes 15 minutes.

WATCHPOINT: Spinach leaves bruise easily so take care when washing and tearing the leaves.

COOK'S TIP: If using dried apricots, use the no-soak variety.

CARROT AND CELERY SALAD

*The addition of quartered hard-cooked eggs will make this
salad into a very substantial first course.*

SERVES 4

2 large carrots
3 sticks celery
1 red pepper
¾ cup walnuts
½ cup corn
1 level tsp paprika
¼ tsp chili powder
4 tbsps oil and vinegar dressing

1. Scrub the carrots and then dice.

2. Slice the celery finely.

3. Remove the core and seeds from the pepper and then dice.

4. Put the carrots, celery and pepper into a serving bowl and add the walnuts and corn.

5. Mix the paprika and chili powder into the dressing and pour over the salad.

6. Mix well and refrigerate for 30 minutes before serving.

TIME: Preparation takes 10 minutes, chilling takes 30 minutes.

SERVING IDEA: Serve as an accompaniment to pasta and grain dishes.

CREAMY MUSHROOM SALAD

Serve this flavorful salad with cold nut roasts, raised pies or quiche.

SERVES 4-6

3 apples
1½ cups celery, diced
4 medium mushrooms
¾ cup walnuts
Lettuce leaves
2 cups alfalfa sprouts
1 cup purple grapes

Dressing
½ cup mayonnaise
¼ cup plain yogurt
Salt and pepper

1. Cut the unpeeled apples into quarters and remove the cores. Dice roughly.

2. Slice the mushrooms thinly.

3. Chop the walnuts roughly.

4. Mix the mayonnaise and yogurt together and season.

5. Put the apples, celery, mushrooms and walnuts into a bowl and fold in the dressing.

6. Line a serving dish with well washed lettuce and spread the sprouts around the outer edge.

7 Pile the salad in the center and garnish with the grapes.

TIME: Preparation takes 15 minutes.

COOK'S TIP: Use red skinned apples and a lettuce tinged with red, such as Lollo Rosso, to give color to your salad.

CRUNCHY CABBAGE SALAD

Serve this very attractive salad for a party or as part of a buffet.

SERVES 4-6

1 large red cabbage
1 green pepper, de-seeded and chopped
½ small pineapple, peeled and finely
  chopped
Segments from 2 medium oranges
6 green onions, finely chopped
3 sticks celery, chopped
½ cup hazelnuts, roughly chopped
½ cup sprouted aduki beans

Dressing
½ cup mayonnaise
¼ cup thick set yogurt
Salt and pepper

1. Remove any tough or discolored outer leaves from the cabbage.

2. Trim the base so that the cabbage will stand upright, and cut about a quarter off the top.

3. Using a sharp knife, scoop out the inside of the cabbage leaving ¼ inch for the shell. Set the shell aside.

4. Discard any tough pieces and shred the remaining cabbage very finely.

5. Put the shredded cabbage into a large bowl together with the pepper, pineapple, orange segments, green onions, celery, hazelnuts and beans.

6. Mix the mayonnaise, yogurt and seasoning together and carefully fold into the vegetables and fruit.

7. Put the mixture into the cabbage shell and place on a serving dish garnished with parsley.

TIME: Preparation takes 20 minutes.

WATCHPOINT: If preparing in advance, refrigerate the salad and dressing separately and mix them together just before serving.

VARIATION: Walnuts may be used in place of hazelnuts but add them when mixing the salad and dressing together.

GREEN PEPPER SALAD

*Serve in individual dishes as an appetizer or
as a light lunch with bread and chunks of cheese.*

SERVES 4-6

3 medium green peppers
3 medium tomatoes
2 medium onions
¾ cup sprouted lentils
Purple grapes for garnish

Dressing
4 tbsps olive oil
2 tbsps red wine vinegar
2 tsps ground cumin
½ tsp fresh coriander, chopped

1. Core and slice the peppers finely.

2. Slice the tomatoes and onions.

3. Arrange the peppers, tomatoes and onions alternately on a round serving dish and sprinkle the lentil sprouts over the top.

4. Mix all the ingredients for the dressing together well and pour over the vegetables.

5. Cover and leave to marinate for at least 1 hour at room temperature before serving.

6. Just before serving, garnish with halved purple grapes.

TIME: Preparation takes 10 minutes. Standing time is 1 hour.

COOK'S TIP: You can prepare this salad in advance and refrigerate until required but remove from the refrigerator 30 minutes before serving.

WATCHPOINT: If growing your own sprouts, make sure you use whole lentils, as red split lentils will not sprout.

Sprouted Lentil Salad

A quick and easy salad.

SERVES 4-6

2 cups broccoli florets
1 red pepper
1 cup sprouted lentils
½ cup golden raisins
4-6 tbsps oil and vinegar dressing
1 tsp freshly grated ginger

1. Cover the broccoli florets with boiling water and leave to stand for 5 minutes. Drain and cool.

2. Core and de-seed the pepper and dice roughly.

3. Arrange the sprouted lentils on a serving dish.

4. Mix together the broccoli, pepper and raisins and pile in the center.

5. Mix the grated ginger with the dressing and pour over the salad.

6. Serve at once.

TIME: Preparation takes 15 minutes.

SERVING IDEA: Serve with pastry based dishes.

VARIATION: Cauliflower florets may be used in place of broccoli.

BROCCOLI AND CAULIFLOWER SALAD

Serve this simple salad with crackers.

SERVES 4

1 red pepper
Small bunch broccoli
Small head of cauliflower
1 tbsp toasted sliced almonds

Dressing
4 tbsps thick set yogurt
2 tbsps lemon juice
2 tbsps olive oil
Salt and pepper
Pinch of nutmeg

1. De-seed the pepper and cut into matchstick pieces.

2. Wash and trim the broccoli and cauliflower and break into small florets.

3. Place the pepper, broccoli and cauliflower in a mixing bowl.

4. Combine the yogurt, lemon juice, olive oil, seasoning and nutmeg in a screw top jar and shake well.

5. Spoon the dressing over the salad and mix together well.

6. Divide the mixture between 4 individual serving plates and garnish with the almond flakes.

TIME: Preparation takes 10 minutes.

VARIATION: Omit the nutmeg from the dressing and add a few freshly chopped herbs.

SPROUTED ADUKI BEAN SALAD

*Serve as an accompaniment to a hot main dish or with cubes
of smoked tofu and lots of crusty French bread for a light luncheon.*

SERVES 4

½ cucumber
1 green pepper
2 cups aduki beansprouts
½ cup toasted peanuts

Dressing
3 tbsps sesame oil
2 tbsps white wine vinegar
1 tbsp shoyu sauce (Japanese soy sauce)
1 tsp brown sugar
Black pepper to taste

1. Chop the cucumber into bite-sized chunks.

2. Cut the pepper in half, de-seed and cut into pieces.

3. Put the cucumber, pepper and beansprouts into a serving dish.

4. Whisk the oil, vinegar, shoyu and sugar together until the sugar has dissolved.

5. Add the pepper to taste.

6. Mix the dressing carefully into the salad and serve at once.

TIME: Preparation takes 10 minutes.

VARIATION: To vary the flavor of the dressing, try walnut oil in place of the sesame oil.

SESAME SPROUT SALAD

Serve as an accompaniment to a hot main dish.

SERVES 4-6

2 medium carrots, peeled
1 green pepper
½ cup dried no-soak apricots
1 tbsp sesame seeds
2 cups beansprouts
4 tbsps oil and vinegar dressing
2 tbsps pineapple juice

1. Cut the carrots into matchsticks.

2. De-seed and slice the pepper thinly.

3. Cut the apricots into slivers.

4. Toast the sesame seeds in a dry pan over a low heat until they are golden brown and give off a delicious aroma.

5. Place the carrots, pepper, apricots and beansprouts in a serving dish.

6. Mix the dressing with the pinapple juice and fold into the salad.

7. Sprinkle the sesame seeds over the top.

8. Serve at once.

TIME: Preparation takes 10 minutes.

COOK'S TIP: Use beansprouts which are at least 1 inch long for this recipe.

PINEAPPLE RICE SALAD

*Serve with stuffed pancakes or simply with crusty
French bread for a light luncheon dish.*

SERVES 4-6

1¼ cups long grain brown rice, cooked
1 cup prepared pineapple, diced
1 bunch green onions, finely chopped
½ cup sliced almonds, lightly toasted
½ bunch radishes, finely sliced
¾ cup beansprouts
Twists of lime for garnish

Dressing
3 tbsps sunflower or safflower oil
1 tbsp sherry
Juice of 1 lime
1 tsp grated ginger root
Salt and pepper

1. Allow the rice to cool.

2. Combine the rice with the pineapple, onions, almonds, radishes and bean sprouts.

3. Mix all the dressing ingredients together.

4. Pour the dressing over the salad and fold in carefully.

5. Refrigerate until required.

6. Garnish with twists of lime.

TIME: Preparation takes 15 minutes, cooking takes 30-35 minutes for the rice.

VARIATION: Use sprouted chickpeas in place of the beansprouts.

116

SMOKED TOFU SALAD

A tasty main course salad. Serve with whole-grain bread.

SEVES 4-6

2 cups broccoli florets
1½ cups mushrooms
4oz can pineapple rings
4 tbsps corn
4-6 tbsps oil and vinegar dressing
1 packet smoked tofu, cut into cubes

1. Cover the broccoli florets with boiling water and leave to stand for 5 minutes. Drain and allow to cool.

2. Wipe the mushrooms with a clean cloth and slice thinly.

3. Cut the pineapple into small pieces.

4. Put the broccoli, mushrooms, pineapple and corn into a large bowl together with the dressing.

5. Mix carefully.

6. Divide the salad between 4 individual dishes and place the smoked tofu on top.

7. Serve at once.

TIME: Preparation takes 15 minutes.

VARIATION: Omit the tofu and serve as a side salad with quiches.

COOK'S TIP: If using plain tofu, marinate for a few hours in equal parts of shoyu sauce and olive oil, together with 1 crushed clove of garlic and 1 tsp of fresh grated ginger.

MAIN MEALS

The main course has traditionally been regarded as the focal point of a meal and the principal source of protein. This is not always the case with a vegetarian meal. For example, pasta alone does not supply enough protein, and nuts or seeds, pulses or some form of dairy produce needs to be added with the pasta or at some other stage in the meal. If a soup containing beans or garnished with grated cheese were followed by a simple pasta dish with a tomato sauce, this would give an adequate supply of protein.

Equally, the same pasta dish followed by a dessert containing milk or eggs would give an equal amount of protein. It is also not always necessary to have one main dish plus two vegetables. Try making smaller portions of one or two main dishes and a couple of appetizers to give variety and provide an interesting and satisfying meal.

Many of the recipes in this section are easy to make and can be prepared in advance if required. Suggested accompaniments are given, but these are only guidelines, and seasonal vegetables should be used when they are at their cheapest and best. A vegetarian main course is generally much cheaper to produce than a meat meal so you can afford to serve a wide range of dishes or to spoil your guests with an exotic dessert.

INDIAN VEGETABLE CURRY

*A wonderfully tasty curry which has the added
advantage of freezing well.*

SERVES 4

Spices
2 tsps turmeric
1 tsp cumin
1 tsp mustard seed
1 tsp fenugreek
4 tsps coriander
½ tsp chili powder
1 tsp ginger
1 tsp black peppercorns

1lb onions, finely chopped
Vegetable oil (vary amount to suit
  – about 4 tbsps)
1¼ cups evaporated milk
2 tbsps white wine vinegar
14oz can tomatoes, processed with
  their juice
1 tbsp tomato paste
2 tsps brown sugar
1 tsp vegetable bouillon powder dissolved
  in little boiling water
4 cups chopped mushrooms or mixed
vegetables (e.g. mushrooms, cauliflower,
carrots, potatoes, okra)

1. Grind all the spices together, this amount will make 3 tbsps of curry powder.

2. Fry the onions in the vegetable oil until golden.

3. Add the ground spices, lower the heat and cook for 3 minutes, stirring all the time.

4. Add the milk and vinegar and stir well.

5. Add the processed tomatoes, tomato paste, sugar and stock.

6. Bring to the boil, cover and simmer very gently for 1 hour.

7. Add the vegetables and cook until tender – about 30 minutes.

TIME: Preparation takes 30 minutes, cooking takes 1 hour 30 minutes.

SERVING IDEA: Serve with boiled brown rice, chappatis or poppadoms and
Cucumber Raita. Cucumber Raita – combine diced cucumber with yogurt, a little
chopped mint, a pinch of chili powder, cumin and seasoning to taste.

FREEZING: The curry sauce will freeze well for up to 3 months so it is well worth while
making double the quantity.

LECSO

A popular recipe from Hungary.

SERVES 4-6

2 medium green peppers
2 medium yellow peppers
1 large onion, finely sliced
2-3 tbsps sunflower oil
2 tbsps paprika
3 medium tomatoes, skinned and
    quartered
2 eggs, well beaten

1. Wash the peppers, core them and cut into strips.

2. Fry the onion in the oil for 1-2 minutes until just colored.

3. Add the paprika, and stir well.

4. Add the peppers and fry for about 2 minutes.

5. Add the tomatoes and fry for a further minute.

6. Add the beaten eggs and seasoning.

7. Stir well until just cooked.

8. Serve immediately on a bed of rice.

TIME: Preparation takes 10 minutes, cooking takes about 10 minutes.

SERVING IDEA: Lecso can be served with boiled potatoes instead of rice.

VARIATION: Red peppers may be used in place of the yellow peppers.

TOFU BURGERS

Serve these delicious burgers with mustard and chutney and accompany with a salad.

MAKES 8

½ cup bulgar wheat
½ cup boiling water
1 small onion, very finely chopped
1 small carrot, grated
¾ cup mushrooms, very finely chopped
9oz package tofu
½ tsp basil
½ tsp oregano
2 tbsps shoyu sauce (Japanese soy sauce)
1 tsp tomato paste
Black pepper
Wholewheat flour
Oil for deep frying

1. Put the bulgar wheat into a bowl and cover with boiling water. Leave to one side for 15 minutes until all the water has been absorbed.

2. Add the onion, carrot and mushrooms to the bulgar and mix well.

3. Drain the tofu and crumble into the bowl.

4. Add the basil, oregano, shoyu, tomato paste, a little black pepper and 1 tablespoon of wholewheat flour. Mix together well.

5. With wet hands, take heaped tablespoonfuls of the mixture, squeeze together well and shape into burgers.

6. Coat the burgers with wholewheat flour.

7. Heat the oil until very hot and fry the burgers 3 or 4 at a time until golden brown.

8. Remove and drain on paper towels.

TIME: Preparation takes 15 minutes, cooking takes 5 minutes per batch.

WATCHPOINT: The oil must be very hot otherwise the burgers will disintegrate.

FREEZING: It is well worth while doubling the quantity and freezing a batch of burgers. Freeze for up to 3 months. Reheat by broiling or warming in the oven.

NUTTY POTATO CAKES

This is the perfect way to use up leftover potatoes.

MAKES 8 CAKES

3 medium potatoes
1 tbsp margarine or butter
A little milk
¾ cup mixed nuts, finely ground
¼ cup sunflower seeds, finely ground
2 tbsps green onions, finely chopped
Freshly ground black pepper
Wholemeal flour for coating
Oil for frying

1. Peel the potatoes, cut into pieces and boil until just soft.

2. Drain and mash with the butter and milk to a creamy consistency.

3. Add the nuts, seeds, onions and pepper to taste.

4. If necessary, add a little more milk at this stage to give a soft texture which holds together.

5. Form into 8 cakes.

6. Coat with flour and fry quickly in as little oil as possible.

7. Drain on paper towels.

8. Serve hot.

TIME: Preparation takes 10 minutes, cooking takes 25 minutes.

SERVING IDEA: Serve with a green salad and sliced tomatoes in an oil and fresh basil dressing.

VARIATION: Dry roast the sunflower seeds until golden brown, before grinding.

CARROT AND CASHEW NUT ROAST

*A delicious roast to serve hot, but the full flavor of
the caraway seeds and lemon are more prominent
when the roast is served cold.*

SERVES 6

1 medium-sized onion, chopped
1-2 cloves garlic, crushed
1 tbsp olive or sunflower oil
2 cups carrots, cooked and mashed
2 cups cashew nuts, ground
1 cup whole-wheat breadcrumbs
1 tbsp light tahini (sesame paste)
1½ tsps caraway seeds
1 tsp yeast extract
Juice of ½ a lemon
⅓ stock from the carrots or water
Salt and pepper

1. Fry the onion and garlic in the oil until soft.

2. Mix together with all the other ingredients and season to taste.

3. Place the mixture in a greased loaf pan.

4. Cover with foil and bake at 350°F for 1 hour.

5. Remove the foil and bake for a further 10 minutes.

6. Leave to stand in the baking pan for at least 10 minutes before turning out.

TIME: Preparation takes 20 minutes, cooking takes 1 hour 10 minutes.

FREEZING: This loaf can be frozen at the end of Step 3. When required, remove
from the freezer and thaw overnight in the refrigerator then continue from
Step 4 or freeze at the end of Step 6.

SERVING IDEA: Serve hot with roast potatoes and a green vegetable, or
cold with a mixed green salad.

STUFFED SQUASH

The perfect use for over large zucchini.

SERVES 4

1 large zucchini
6 tbsps fresh whole-wheat breadcrumbs
2-4 tbsps milk
4 eggs, hard-cooked
1 cup grated cheese
Salt and pepper
Pinch of freshly grated nutmeg
1 egg, beaten
A little margarine or butter
Parsley and 1 red pepper for garnish

1. Wash the zucchini well, cut in half lengthwise and scoop out inside, leaving a thick shell.

2. Place in a well greased pan or baking dish.

3. Soak the breadcrumbs in the milk.

4. Chop the hard-cooked eggs and add to the breadcrumbs together with the cheese, seasoning and nutmeg.

5. Bind the mixture with the beaten egg.

6. Pile into the zucchini halves and dot with knobs of margarine or butter.

7. Pour a little water around the zucchini and bake in a moderate oven, 375°F for 35-40 minutes until the zucchini is tender and the top is nicely browned. (If the top is browning too quickly, cover with foil.)

8. Serve on a large dish garnished with parsley and red pepper rings.

TIME: Preparation takes 25 minutes, cooking takes 35-40 minutes.

SERVING IDEA: For a special occasion garnish with cranberries and surround with sliced red or yellow peppers, chopped lettuce and watercress.

VARIATION: Other squash like butternut or acorn may be substituted.

INDIAN STYLE ZUCCHINI

*Cumin and fennel give a whole new
flavor to this popular vegetable.*

SERVES 4

4 medium zucchini
2 tbsps olive oil
1 onion, very finely chopped
2 small carrots, grated
½ tsp paprika
1 tsp cumin seeds
¼ tsp turmeric
¼ tsp fennel seeds
½ cup flaked coconut

1. Wash the zucchini and cut in half lengthwise.

2. Using a teaspoon, remove the flesh leaving about ¼ inch shell.

3. Chop the flesh finely.

4. Heat the oil and sauté the onion for a few minutes.

5. Add the carrots, zucchini flesh and spices and cook, stirring frequently, for a further 5 minutes until softened.

6. Remove from the heat and stir in the coconut.

7. Divide the mixture between the zucchini shells mounding it slightly.

8. Place in a greased ovenproof casserole and bake at 375°F for 45 minutes until the zucchini shells are soft.

9. Serve immediately.

TIME: Preparation takes 10 minutes, cooking takes 55 minutes.

SERVING IDEA: Mix plain yogurt with some finely chopped mint or coriander (cilantro) and a squeeze of lemon juice. Serve as a sauce.

TASTY TOMATO SAUCE

*Serve this adaptable sauce over stuffed
eggplant, zucchini or peppers.*

SERVES 4

¼ cup pine kernels
Pinch of salt
1 tsp sunflower oil
1 onion, peeled and chopped
Pinch of chili powder
3 cloves
14oz can tomatoes

1. Place the pine kernels in a frying pan and dry roast. Remove when they are lightly browned and sprinkle with the salt.

2. Fry the onion in the sunflower oil until soft.

3. Add the chili powder and cloves. Fry for 1 minute.

4. Add the tomatoes, bring to the boil and simmer for 10 minutes.

5. Cool slightly and remove the cloves.

6. Blend the mixture in a food processor and return to pan. Add the pine kernels and gently reheat.

TIME: Preparation takes 10 minutes, cooking takes 15 minutes.

WATCHPOINT: Dry roast the pine kernels over a low heat, stirring continuously, otherwise they will burn.

Butter Bean Roast

*A combination of simple ingredients makes this
a useful recipe for mid-week meals.*

SERVES 4

1 cup dried butter beans
2 large onions
A little oil for frying
2 cups mushrooms, sliced
1 cup cooked rice
1 egg, beaten
1 tbsp freshly chopped parsley
1 tsp dried mixed herbs
Salt and pepper

1. Soak the beans overnight, change the water and cook until soft – about 1-1¼ hours.

2. Drain and mash the beans thoroughly.

3. Slice the onions finely and fry in a little oil until golden brown, adding the mushrooms after 10 minutes.

4. Mix all the ingredients together in a bowl.

5. Place the mixture in a greased 1lb loaf pan and bake at 375°F for 30 minutes or until browned on top.

TIME: Preparation takes 10-15 minutes, bean cooking takes 1-1¼ hours, and cooking takes 30 minutes for roast.

SERVING IDEA: Serve with potatoes and salad.

FREEZING: Prepare to the end of Step 4. Place the mixture in the loaf pan, cover with foil and freeze for up to 2 months. To de-frost, remove from freezer 8 hours before required and allow to defrost at room temperature. Cook as above.

PERFECT POTATOES

*Potatoes become extra special when teamed
up with the flavor of onion.*

SERVES 5

6 medium potatoes
1 large onion
Salt and pepper
1¼ cups milk
1½ tbsps butter or margarine

1. Peel and finely slice the potatoes and onion.

2. Layer the potato slices and onion in a shallow ovenproof dish, sprinkling each layer with some salt and pepper.

3. Pour over the milk and dot with the butter or margarine.

4. Bake uncovered in a preheated oven, 350°F for 1-1½ hours or until the potatoes are soft, golden and brown on top.

TIME: Preparation takes 15 minutes, cooking takes 1-1½ hours.

SERVING IDEA: Serve with broiled mushrooms and tomatoes for a supper dish or serve with roasts, burgers or pies.

FREEZING: Cook quickly, cover with foil and place in a freezer bag. Thaw at room temperature for 4-6 hours and reheat at 375°F for about 30 minutes.

VARIATION: Place a layer of finely sliced cooking apples in the bottom of the dish.

VALENCIA LOAF

This loaf is delicious served with apple sauce and a variety of vegetables.

SERVES 6

---

2 large onions
⅓ cup.oil
3oz spaghetti
½ cup whole-wheat breadcrumbs
2 cups ground almonds
2 eggs, beaten
1 tsp sage
Rind and juice of 1 lemon
Salt and pepper

---

1. Peel and slice the onions and fry in the oil for 10 minutes over a low heat.

2. Cook the spaghetti in boiling, salted water until *al dente*.

3. Drain the spaghetti and add the onion, breadcrumbs, almonds, eggs, sage, lemon juice and rind. Season to taste.

4. Stir carefully and put into a greased 9 x 5 inch loaf pan, lined with waxpaper.

5. Cover and bake in a moderate oven 375°F for 1 hour.

6. Turn out onto a serving dish and remove the lining paper carefully.

7. Cut into thick slices and serve immediately.

TIME: Preparation takes 15 minutes, cooking takes 1 hour 20 minutes.

VARIATION: ½ cup of soy flour mixed with a little water may be used in place of the eggs.

143

DEEP MUSHROOM PIE

A delicious pie and so adaptable. Serve with
salad or potatoes and a green vegetable.

SERVES 4

Filling
1 tbsp vegetable oil
4½ cups mushrooms, cleaned and
    chopped
2 cups mixed nuts, finely milled
2 medium onions, peeled and finely
    chopped
1 cup whole-wheat breadcrumbs
2 eggs, beaten
1 tsp dried thyme or 2 tsps fresh
1 tsp dried marjoram or 2 tsps fresh
1 tbsps shoyu (Japanese soy sauce)
Salt and pepper to taste
Small quantity of stock to achieve right
    consistency if necessary

Crust
3 cups whole-wheat flour
Pinch of salt
1 tsp baking powder (optional)
½ cup solid vegetable shortening
½ cup water plus extra boiling water
    as necessary
Beaten egg to glaze

1. Heat the oil in a large saucepan and gently fry the onion until soft.

2. Add the finely chopped mushrooms and cook until the juices begin to run.

3. Remove from the heat and add all the other filling ingredients to form a thick, but not dry, consistency adding a little stock or water if necessary. Allow to cool.

4. To prepare the dough, first sift the flour, salt and baking powder into a large mixing bowl.

5. Cut the shortening into small pieces and melt in a saucepan. Add the cold water and bring to a fierce, rolling boil.

6. Immediately pour into the center of the flour and mix vigorously with a wooden spoon until glossy.

7. When the mixture is cool enough to handle, use hands and knead it into a ball.

8. Divide the mixture into two-thirds and one-third, placing the one-thirds portion in an oiled plastic bag to prevent drying out.

9. Use the two-thirds portion to line the base and sides of a 7 inch spring form pan, pressing it down and moulding it into position.

10. Spoon in the mushroom filling, press down firmly making a "dome" shape.

11. Roll out the remaining dough to just larger than the pan and place on top of the pie, pinching the edges together to seal.

12. Trim off excess dough and glaze generously with beaten egg.

13. Cut or prick vents in the lid to allow the steam to escape.

14. Bake at 425°F for 20 minutes. Reduce to 375°F and bake for a further hour.

15. Unmold and serve on an attractive platter garnished with parsley and twists of lemon and cucumber.

TIME: Preparation takes about 35 minutes, cooking takes 1 hour 20 minutes.

SPINACH, CORN AND NUT PIE

An attractive pie which is suitable for family meals and entertaining.

SERVES 6

1lb spinach
1 onion, chopped
2 tbsps oil
1 cup hazelnuts, finely chopped
1 cup brazil nuts, finely chopped
1 cup wholemeal breadcrumbs
⅔ cup corn
1 tsp oregano
½ tsp sage
1 tbsp freshly chopped parsley
1 tsp shoyu (Japanese soy sauce)
2 tbsps tahini (sesame paste)
1¼ cups stock
Salt and pepper

Crust
3 cups whole-wheat flour
1 tsp baking powder
½ cup vegetable fat
¾ cup water
Pinch of salt

1. Steam the spinach until soft. Drain well and chop finely.

2. Fry the onion in the oil until soft.

3. Mix together all the dry ingredients, add the shoyu, tahini and sufficient stock to give a moist texture.

4. Season to taste.

5. For the dough, mix together the dry ingredients.

6. Melt the fat in the water and heat until about to boil.

7. Add the liquid to the flour and mix well. Add extra boiling water if the mixture is too dry.

8. Put two thirds of the dough into a 7 inch spring form pan and push into shape.

9. Put the filling into the pie case and press down well.

10. Roll out the remaining dough and make a pie lid.

11. Glaze the top and make two small steam holes.

12. Bake at 425°F for 20 minutes, reduce the heat to 375°F for a further 50 minutes or until golden brown.

TIME: Preparation takes about 40 minutes, cooking takes about 1 hour 15 minutes.

SERVING IDEA: Serve hot with vegetables or cold with salad.

COOK'S TIP: There is no need to grease the pan when using hot water dough.

CORN AND PARSNIP QUICHE

Serve this unusual quiche with jacket potatoes
filled with cottage cheese and chives.

SERVES 6

Crust
⅓ cup whipped margarine
1½ cups whole-wheat flour
1 tsp baking powder
Pinch of salt
4-6 tbsps ice-cold water
1 tbsp oil

Filling
1 large onion, peeled and finely chopped
1 clove garlic, crushed
2 tbsps butter or margarine
2 large parsnips, steamed and roughly
    mashed
1 cup corn, frozen or canned
1 tsp dried basil
Salt and pepper
3 eggs
⅔ cup milk
¾ cup grated cheddar cheese
1 medium tomato, sliced

1. Rub the margarine into the flour, baking powder and salt until the mixture resembles fine breadcrumbs.

2. Add the water and oil and work together lightly. The mixture should be fairly moist.

3. Leave for half an hour.

4. Roll out and line a 10 inch pie dish.

5. Prick the bottom and bake blind at 425°F for about 8 minutes.

6. Meanwhile, sauté the onion and garlic in the butter or margarine until soft and golden.

7. Add the parsnips, corn and basil and season to taste.

8. Beat the eggs and add the milk.

9. Add to the vegetable mixture and stir over a low heat until the mixture just begins to set.

10. Pour into the dough and top with the grated cheese and sliced tomato.

11. Bake 375°F for 15-20 minutes or until the cheese is golden brown.

TIME: Preparation takes about 40 minutes, cooking takes 30 minutes.

COOK'S TIP: The partial cooking of the whole mixture helps to keep the crust from becoming soggy and considerably reduces the cooking time.

RATATOUILLE PIE WITH CHEESE AND PEANUT PASTRY

*A colorful dish to make when eggplants
and zucchini are cheap and plentiful.*

SERVES 4-6

Ratatouille
2 tbsps olive oil
2 onions, chopped
4 tomatoes, sliced
1 eggplant, sliced
3 zucchini, finely sliced
2 sticks celery, chopped

White sauce
4 tbsps flour
4 tbsps margarine
Scant 2 cups milk

Crust
4 tbsps butter
1 cup self-rising flour
4 tbsps finely grated cheese
½ cup finely chopped salted peanuts
A little milk
Beaten egg

1. Put the oil and all the vegetables into a large pan and cook gently for about 20 minutes or until soft.

2. To make the sauce, melt the margarine in a separate pan, stir in the flour and cook for 2 minutes, stirring all the time.

3. Gradually add most of the milk and bring to boiling point. Add remaining milk if needed

4. Stir the sauce into the vegetable mixture and put into an ovenproof dish.

5. Rub the butter into the flour and add the cheese and peanuts.

6. Add a little milk and roll out the dough.

7. Place on top of the ratatouille mixture, trim and brush with beaten egg.

8. Bake 375°F for about 30 minutes or until golden brown.

TIME: Preparation takes 30 minutes, cooking takes 1 hour.

SERVING IDEA: Serve with bundles of julienne vegetables – carrots, rutabaga, turnips etc.

VARIATION: Sliced green pepper can be used in place of the celery.

Sweet Potato and Green Bean Turnovers

These savory pies are a tasty addition to any lunch box or picnic basket.

SERVES 4

Wholemeal dough for a 10 inch single
   crust pie
½ medium onion, finely chopped
1 clove garlic, crushed
1 tbsp oil
½ tsp freshly grated ginger
¼ – ½ tsp chili powder
¼ tsp turmeric
½ tsp ground cumin
1 tsp ground coriander
¼ tsp mustard powder
1 medium-sized sweet potato, cooked and
   finely diced
½ cup green beans, chopped into ½ inch
   lengths
2 tbsps water or stock
Salt and pepper

1. Fry the onion and garlic in the oil until soft.

2. Add the ginger and all the spices and stir.

3. Add the diced potato, beans and water or stock and cook gently for 4-5 minutes or until the beans begin to cook.

4. Allow the mixture to cool and season well.

5. Roll out the dough into 4 circles.

6. Place a quarter of the filling in the center of each circle and dampen the edges of the dough with a little water.

7. Join the dough together over the filling.

8. Make a small hole in each pie and glaze with milk or egg.

9. Bake for 15-20 minutes at 400°F.

TIME: Preparation, including making the dough, takes 25 minutes.
Cooking takes 15-20 minutes.

FREEZING: The pies will freeze well for up to 2 months. Thaw at room temperature.

153

NUTTY SPAGHETTI

An easy-to-make lunch or supper dish.

SERVES 4

8oz spaghetti
3½ cups boiling, salted water
1 onion, finely chopped
2 tbsps sunflower oil
2½ tsps curry powder
¾ cup tomato juice
3 tbsps crunchy peanut butter
1 tbsp lemon juice
Lemon twists and peanuts for garnish

1. Boil the spaghetti until just tender and drain well.

2. Fry the onion in the oil until golden brown.

3. Stir in the curry powder, tomato juice, peanut butter and lemon juice.

4. Simmer for 5 minutes and then stir into the spaghetti.

TIME: Preparation takes about 10 minutes, cooking takes 25 minutes.

SERVING IDEA: Serve garnished with lemon twists and peanuts.

VARIATION: Almond butter and blanched almonds can be used in place of the peanut butter and peanuts.

CONCHIGLIE WITH TWO SAUCES

A very low fat pasta dish with two delicious sauces.

SERVES 4

1lb cooked conchiglie (pasta shells)

Tomato sauce
1 large onion, very finely chopped
1 tsp bouillon powder
3 tbsps water
1 clove garlic, crushed
½ tsp dried thyme
Pinch ground rosemary
14oz can tomatoes

Mushroom sauce
3½ cups oyster mushrooms
2 tbsps low fat margarine
1 tsp bouillon powder
4 tbsps thick set plain yogurt
Chopped parsley for garnish

---

1. To make the tomato sauce, place the onion, bouillon powder, water and garlic in a pan and cook very gently for 7-10 minutes until the onion is soft.

2. Add the thyme and rosemary and cook for 1 minute.

3. Chop the canned tomatoes and add to the pan together with the tomato juice.

4. Bring to the boil and boil rapidly until the sauce has reduced and thickened.

5. To make the mushroom sauce, chop the mushrooms finely.

6. Melt the margarine in a pan and add the bouillon powder and mushrooms.

7. Simmer very gently for 10-15 minutes.

8. Remove from the heat and stir in the yogurt.

9. Heat gently until hot but do not boil.

10. Divide the pasta between 4 serving dishes and pour the tomato sauce over one half of the pasta and the mushroom sauce over the other side of the pasta.

11. Sprinkle over the chopped parsley.

12. Serve at once.

TIME: Preparation takes 20 minutes, cooking, including the pasta, takes 35 minutes.

COOK'S TIP: The sauces may be prepared in advance, refrigerated and reheated when required.

VARIATION: Fresh pasta is best but any pasta can be used and both sauces are suitable for use on their own – just double the quantities given.

ZUCCHINI AND CARROT LAYER

*Serve with a sprouted salad for a light lunch or glaze
with agar and fresh herbs for a special occasion.*

SERVES 4

7-8 carrots, cooked, mashed and
    seasoned
1 medium onion
3 cups zucchini, finely chopped
1 tbsp oil
1 cup almonds, finely chopped or
    ground
¾ cup whole-wheat breadcrumbs
1 tsp vegetable bouillon dissolved in
    a little boiling water
1 egg, beaten
1 level tsp mixed herbs
1 tbsp tomato paste
1 tbsps shoyu sauce (Japanese soy sauce)
Ground black pepper

1. Grease and line a 7½ x 4inch loaf pan.

2. Fry the onion and zucchini in the oil, add all the remaining ingredients except the carrot, and mix together well.

3. Place half of the zucchini mixture into the loaf pan and press down well.

4. Arrange the carrots on top of this followed by the remaining zucchini mixture.

5. Cover with foil and cook for 1 hour at 350°F.

6. Allow to cool for 10 minutes before removing from pan.

TIME: Preparation, including cooking the carrots, takes 25 minutes.

COOK'S TIP: This mixture makes a delicious filling for a pie.

ZUCCHINI AND CORN SAVORY

This is an excellent way to use up leftover pasta.

SERVES 4

1 tbsp oil
1 medium onion, chopped
1½ cups zucchini, sliced
1⅓ cups corn
1½-2 cups cooked pasta shapes
Large pinch oregano
1 tbsp tomato paste
Salt and pepper

Sauce
2 tbsps margarine
2 tbsps whole-wheat flour
1¼ cups skimmed milk
3 tbsps white wine
½ cup strong flavored cheese, grated

Topping
¼ cup whole-wheat breadcrumbs
1 dstsp sunflower seeds

1. Heat the oil in a frying pan and sauté the chopped onion until soft.

2. Add the sliced zucchini and brown lightly.

3. Mix in the corn, cooked pasta, oregano and tomato paste, and stir.

4. Season lightly and transfer the mixture to an oiled ovenproof dish.

5. Make the cheese sauce by melting the margarine and stirring in the flour to make a roux. Cook gently for a few minutes and then pour on the milk and wine, stirring all the time, to make a smooth sauce.

6. Add the grated cheese and stir until it melts into the sauce. Remove from the heat and pour over the vegetable mixture.

7. Top with the breadcrumbs and sunflower seeds.

8. Bake 350°F for about 20 minutes until the dish is brown and bubbling.

TIME: Preparation takes about 30 minutes, cooking takes 20 minutes.

SERVING IDEA: Serve with broiled tomatoes and a green salad.

VEGETABLE CRISP

*A variety of hearty vegetables topped with oats and
cheese makes the perfect winter meal.*

SERVES 4-6

Topping
⅓ cup butter or margarine
1 cup whole-wheat flour
½ cup rolled oatmeal
1 cup cheddar cheese, grated
¼ tsp salt

¾ cup stock or water
1¼ cups apple cider
1 tsp brown sugar
2 carrots, chopped
2 large parsnips, cut into rings
2 sticks celery, chopped
2 heads broccoli, cut into florets
¼ cauliflower, cut into florets
2 tsps whole-wheat flour
2 tbsps chopped parsley
1 medium onion, chopped and fried until
  golden
4 large tomatoes, peeled and sliced
1 cup cooked black-eyed peas
Salt and pepper

1. Make the topping by rubbing the butter
into the flour and oats until the mixture
resembles breadcrumbs.

2. Stir in the cheese and salt.

3. Mix the stock with the cider and sugar
and put into a large pan with the carrots
and parsnips.

4. Cook until just tender, remove the
vegetables and put aside.

5. Add the celery, broccoli and cauliflower
to the pan, cook until tender, remove and
reserve with other vegetables.

6. Mix the flour with a little water, add to
the cider and cook until thickened, stirring
all the time.

7. Cook for 2-3 minutes, remove from the
heat and add the parsley.

8. Place the onions, vegetables, tomatoes
and beans in a greased casserole dish and
season well. Pour the sauce over the
mixture.

9. Sprinkle the topping over the top and
press down a little.

10. Cook at 400°F for 30-35 minutes or
until the topping is golden brown.

TIME: Preparation takes 20 minutes, cooking takes 1 hour 5 minutes.

SERVING IDEA: Serve with roast potatoes.

COOK'S TIP: The casserole can be prepared in advance to the end of Step 9.
Refrigerate until ready to cook.

RATATOUILLE LASAGNE

*Serve with rolls and a green salad
for the perfect lunch or supper.*

SERVES 4-6

6 strips spinach lasagne verdi or
   wholemeal lasagne
2-3 tbsps olive oil
2 onions, finely chopped
2 cloves garlic, crushed
1 large eggplant, chopped
1 zucchini, sliced thinly
1 green pepper, chopped
1 red pepper, chopped
14oz can tomatoes, chopped
2-3 tbsps tomato paste
A little vegetable stock
Salt and freshly ground black pepper

White sauce
2 tbsps butter or margarine
2 tbsps whole-wheat flour
1¼ cups milk

⅓ cup Parmesan cheese, grated
Parsley, to garnish

1. Preheat the oven to 350°F.

2. Cook the lasagne in boiling, salted water for 12-15 minutes.

3. Plunge pasta into a bowl of cold water to prevent overcooking or sticking.

4. Heat the oil and fry the onion and garlic until soft.

5. Add the eggplant, zucchini and peppers and sauté until soft.

6. Add the tomatoes with their juice and the tomato paste and simmer until tender. It may be necessary to add a little stock at this stage.

7. Season well and set aside.

8. Make the white sauce by melting the butter in a small saucepan.

9. Add the flour and cook to a roux.

10. Add the milk slowly, stirring constantly, bring to the boil and simmer for about 5 minutes. Remove from the heat.

11. Grease a deep ovenproof dish.

12. Layer the ratatouille and lasagne strips, starting with the ratatouille and finishing with a layer of lasagne.

13. Pour over the white sauce and sprinkle the Parmesan cheese over the top.

14. Bake in the oven for 35 minutes until golden. Garnish with parsley before serving.

TIME: Preparation takes about 20 minutes, cooking takes 1 hour.

VARIATION: If eggplant is not available, 3 cups sliced mushrooms may be used instead.

SAVORY BEAN POT

Serve this exciting mixture with rice or baked potatoes and a salad.

SERVES 4

2 tbsps vegetable oil
2 vegetable bouillon cubes, crumbled
2 medium onions, chopped
2 apples, peeled and grated
2 medium carrots, grated
3 tbsps tomato paste
1¼ cups water
2 tbsps white wine vinegar
1 tbsp dried mustard
1 level tsp oregano
1 level tsp cumin
2 tsps brown sugar
Salt and pepper
3 cups cooked red kidney beans
A little sour cream

1. Heat the oil in a non-stick pan.

2. Add the crumbled bouillon cubes, onions, apples and carrots.

3. Sauté for 5 minutes, stirring continuously.

4. Mix the tomato paste with the water and add together with all the other ingredients apart from the beans and cream.

5. Stir well, cover and simmer for 2 minutes.

6. Add the beans and spoon the mixture into an ovenproof casserole.

7. Cover and cook at 350°F for 35-40 minutes.

8. Add a little more water after 20 minutes if necessary.

9. Top with swirls of sour cream and serve.

TIME: Preparation takes 20 minutes, cooking takes 45 minutes.

VARIATION: Use cider vinegar in place of the white wine vinegar.

VEGETABLE STEW WITH HERB DUMPLINGS

The ideal meal to warm up a cold winter's night.

SERVE 4-6

1 large onion
5 cups mixed vegetables (carrot, rutabaga,
   parsnips, turnips, cauliflower etc.)
2½ cups stock or water plus a stock cube
Salt and pepper
Flour or proprietory gravy powder to
   thicken

Dumplings
1 cup whole-wheat flour
2 tsps baking powder
¼ cup vegetable shortening
1 tsp mixed herbs
¼ tsp salt

1. Chop the onion into large pieces.

2. Peel and prepare the vegetables and chop into bite-sized pieces.

3. Put the onion and vegetables into a pan and cover with the stock.

4. Bring to the boil and simmer for 20 minutes.

5. Season to taste.

6. Mix a little flour with a little water and stir into the stew to thicken. Add more, if needed.

7. Place the ingredients for the dumplings into a bowl and rub together until they resemble breadcrumbs. Add just enough water to bind.

8. Shape the mixture into 8 small dumplings.

9. Bring the stew to the boil and drop in the dumplings.

10. Cover and allow to simmer for 10 minutes or until dumplings are light and tender.

11. Serve at once.

TIME: Preparation takes 10 minutes, cooking takes 30 minutes.

SERVING IDEA: Serve with boiled potatoes.

VARIATION: The mixed herbs may be omitted when making the dumplings or chopped fresh parsley and a squeeze of lemon juice may be used instead.

MUSHROOM STROGANOFF

A great favorite which is much appreciated by all age groups.

SERVES 4-6

2 medium onions, sliced
5 sticks celery, chopped
4 tbsps butter or margarine
6 cups small mushrooms
½ tsp mixed herbs
½ tsp basil
1 heaped tbsp unbleached flour
1¼ cups stock
Salt and pepper
⅓ cup sour cream or plain yogurt
Chopped parsley

1. Put the onions and celery into a large pan together with the butter or margarine and sauté over a low heat until the onions are transparent.

2. Add the mushrooms and cook for 2-3 minutes until the juices run.

3. Add the mixed herbs and basil.

4. Stir in the flour and cook for 1 minute.

5. Add the stock and seasoning and allow to cook gently for 8-10 minutes.

6. Remove from the heat, stir in the sour cream and adjust the seasoning if necessary.

7. Heat very gently to serving temperature but do not allow to boil.

8. Garnish with the chopped parsley and serve at once.

TIME: Preparation takes 10 minutes, cooking takes 20 minutes.

SERVING IDEA: Serve on a bed of Walnut Rice – cook enough rice to serve 4-6 people and carefully fold in seasoning, a little butter, 1 crushed clove of garlic and ½ cup finely chopped walnuts.

COOK'S TIP: If small mushrooms are not available use the larger variety and slice thickly or quarter.

Fifteen Minute Goulash

This quick and easy goulash is delicious served with baked potatoes or noodles.

SERVES 4

1 onion, finely chopped
1 clove garlic, crushed
2 carrots, diced
3 medium zucchini, diced
2 tbsps olive oil
1 tbsp paprika
Pinch of nutmeg
1 heaped tbsp freshly chopped parsley
1 tbsp tomato paste
14oz can tomatoes
1½ cups cooked red kidney beans or 14oz can, drained and rinsed
1½ cups cooked white kidney beans or 14oz can, drained and washed
⅔ cup tomato juice or stock
Salt and pepper
Sour cream or plain yogurt to serve

1. Put the onion, garlic, carrots and zucchini into a pan with the olive oil and sauté for 5 minutes until softened.

2. Stir in the paprika, nutmeg, parsley and tomato paste.

3. Add the rest of the ingredients except sour cream or yogurt and cook over a low heat for 10 minutes.

4. Turn onto a hot serving dish and top with a little sour cream or yogurt.

TIME: Preparation takes 10 minutes, cooking takes 15 minutes.

VARIATION: Vary the type of bean used – try navy, soy beans or even chick peas.

BISCUIT BASED PIZZA

Just the right pizza for four hungry people.

SERVES 4

Base
⅓ cup margarine
1¾ cups whole-wheat flour
2 small eggs plus 2 tbsps milk or 4 tbsps
    soy flour mixed with 3 tbsps water
½ tsp mixed herbs
½ tsp dried mustard
Salt and pepper

Topping
A little olive oil
1 tbsp tomato paste
¼ cup margarine
1 large onion, finely chopped
1 cup mushrooms, sliced
1 green or red pepper, finely sliced
4 tomatoes, sliced
2 sticks celery, finely sliced
1 cup cheddar cheese, grated

1. Make the biscuit mix by rubbing the margarine into the flour until it resembles fine breadcrumbs.

2. Beat the eggs together with the milk.

3. Add to the flour mixture together with the herbs, mustard and seasoning. Knead together to form a ball of dough.

4. Press the mixture evenly over a 10 inch pizza pan.

5. Brush the top with a little olive oil and spread the tomato paste evenly over the top with a knife.

6. Melt the margarine in a frying pan and cook the onions, mushrooms, pepper and celery for 4-5 minutes until softened a little.

7. Pile the mixture on top of the pizza base.

8. Lay the tomatoes evenly over the top and sprinkle on the grated cheese.

9. Bake for 20-25 minutes at 400°F until the cheese is melted and golden brown and the base is crisp.

TIME: Preparation takes 20 minutes, cooking takes about 30 minutes.

SERVING IDEA: Garnish with watercress and serve with a crisp green salad.

FREEZING: Freeze after cooking for up to 2 months. Allow to thaw before reheating in the oven.

EXPRESS VEGETABLE PIE

*Any cooked, leftover vegetables may be
used for this quick and easy pie.*

SERVES 4

1 large onion, peeled and finely chopped
2 tbsps margarine
2 sticks of celery, diced
¾ cup cashew nuts, chopped and dry
  roasted
4 cups mixed frozen vegetables (peas,
  corn, rutabaga, carrot, turnip, diced
  peppers, parsnip etc.)
2 tsps tomato paste
⅔ cup water or stock
½ -1 tsp yeast extract
Salt and black pepper
3-4 large potatoes
1 tbsp butter
A little milk

1. Sauté the onion in the margarine
together with the celery and a little water
until just tender.

2. Add the remaining ingredients apart
from the potatoes, butter and milk.

3. Simmer for 3-5 minutes, adding a little
more water if the mixture seems too dry.
Keep hot.

4. Cook the potatoes until soft, mash with
butter and a little milk, adding salt and
pepper to taste.

5. Turn the vegetable mixture into a
casserole dish and cover completely with
the mashed potato.

6. Fork over the top roughly, dot with
butter and broil for 3-5 minutes until
golden brown.

7. Serve immediately.

TIME: Preparation takes 20 minutes, cooking takes 15 minutes.

SERVING IDEA: Serve with salad, mushrooms and pumpkin seeds.

SAVORY RICE CAKE

An excellent way to use up leftover rice.

SERVES 2-4

1 medium onion, finely chopped
1 clove garlic, crushed
2 tbsps olive oil
1 tbsp fresh thyme, chopped
1 red pepper, thinly sliced
1 green pepper, thinly sliced
4 eggs, beaten
Salt and pepper
6 tbsps cooked brown rice
3 tbsps plain yogurt
¾ cup cheddar cheese, grated

1. Fry the onion and garlic in the olive oil until soft.

2. Add the thyme and pepper and fry gently for 4-5 minutes.

3. Beat the eggs with the salt and pepper.

4. Add the cooked rice to the thyme and pepper followed by the eggs.

5. Cook over a moderate heat, stirring from time to time until the eggs are cooked underneath.

6. Spoon the yogurt on top of the part-set egg and sprinkle the cheese over the top.

7. Put under a moderate broiler and cook until puffed and golden.

8. Serve immediately.

TIME: Preparation takes about 15 minutes, cooking takes 15 minutes.

SERVING IDEA: Garnish with fresh thyme and serve with a green salad.

QUICK VEGETABLE CHILI

Serve this tasty chili with whole-wheat rolls and salad.

SERVES 4

2 large onions, sliced
1 tbsp olive oil
1 small clove garlic, crushed
1 tsp chili powder
14oz can tomatoes, chopped
14oz can of red kidney beans
1 small red pepper, roughly chopped
1 medium zucchini, sliced into chunks
Cauliflower florets
2 carrots, roughly chopped
½ tbsp tomato paste
1 tsp dried, sweet basil
1 tsp oregano
¾-1 cup stock

1. Sauté the onions in the oil until soft.

2. Add the garlic and cook for 1 minute.

3. Add the chili powder and cook for a further minute.

4. Add the rest of the ingredients and simmer for 25-30 minutes.

5. Serve on a bed of brown rice.

TIME: Preparation takes about 15 minutes, cooking takes 30 minutes.

VARIATION: Broccoli florets could be used in place of the cauliflower.

Speedy Pizza

The perfect meal in a hurry.

SERVES 4-6

Dough
2 cups whole-wheat flour
4 tsps baking powder
⅓ cup shortening
Scant ½ tsp salt
Cold water to mix, approx. 1 cup

Filling
Olive oil
1 tbsp tomato paste
1 medium onion, very finely chopped
14oz can artichokes, halved
6 medium tomatoes, skinned and sliced
1 tsp dried oregano
1 cup Mozzarella cheese, finely sliced
12 black olives, stoned and halved
  (optional)

1. Rub the flour, salt and shortening together mixture resembles breadcrumbs. Add enough cold water to make a pliable dough.

2. Roll out into a 10-inch circle and place on a greased baking sheet.

3. Brush with olive oil and cover with the tomato paste.

4. Arrange the onion, artichokes and tomatoes on the top.

5. Sprinkle with oregano.

6. Arrange the cheese evenly over the top and add the olives.

7. Bake at 375°F for about 35 minutes.

TIME: Preparation takes 10 minutes, cooking takes 35 minutes.

SERVING IDEA: Serve with a crisp salad.

VARIATION: Zucchini or mushrooms may be used in place of the artichokes.
Basil or mixed herbs can take the place of the oregano.

WATCHPOINT: Make sure that you chop the onions very finely or they will not cook.
Alternatively, if you have time, you can pre-cook the onions a little
before putting on top of the pizza.

ZUCCHINI MEDITERRANEAN STYLE

*Zucchini originally came from Italy, so why
not give them the continental treatment!*

SERVES 4

---

3 tbsps olive oil
1 large onion, finely chopped
3 cloves garlic, crushed
1 red pepper, chopped
1 cup cooked navy beans
14oz can tomatoes
3 cups zucchini, finely sliced
1 level tsp oregano
Seasoning

1. Heat the oil in a pan.

2. Add the onion, garlic and pepper and cook for 4-5 minutes.

3. Add the cooked beans, canned tomatoes and zucchini. Stir well.

4. Add the oregano and seasoning, and stir again.

5. Cover and cook slowly for 30 minutes.

TIME: Preparation takes 10-15 minutes, cooking takes 40 minutes.

SERVING IDEA: Serve on a bed of white rice.

COOK'S TIP: This dish will reheat well.

OVEN BAKED SPAGHETTI

A convenient way to cook this favorite mid-week meal.

SERVES 4

8oz whole-wheat spaghetti, cooked
2 x 14oz cans tomatoes, roughly
 chopped
1 large onion, grated
1 tsp oregano
Seasoning
1 cup Gruyere cheese, sliced
2 tbsps Parmesan cheese, grated

1. Grease four individual ovenproof dishes and place a quarter of the spaghetti in each one.

2. Pour the tomatoes over the top.

3. Add the onion, sprinkle with oregano and season well.

4. Arrange the sliced cheese over the top of the spaghetti mixture.

5. Sprinkle with Parmesan and bake at 350°F for 30 minutes.

TIME: Preparation takes 10 minutes, cooking takes 20-25 minutes.

SERVING IDEA: Serve with garlic bread.

WATCHPOINT: When cooking spaghetti remember to add a few drops of oil to the boiling water to stop it sticking together.

COOK'S TIP: Oven Baked Spaghetti may be cooked in one large casserole if required but add 10 minutes to the cooking time.

TOMATO AND PEPPER QUICHE

Make quiche a more filling meal with a selection of salads.

SERVES 4

Crust
1 cup whole-wheat flour
Pinch of salt
¼ cup vegetable fat
A little cold water to mix

Filling
2 tbsps butter or margarine
1 onion, finely chopped
½ green pepper, finely sliced
½ red pepper, finely sliced
2 tomatoes, finely sliced
3 eggs
1¼ cups cream
Seasoning
2 tbsps Parmesan cheese

1. Mix the flour and salt together.

2. Cut the fat into small pieces and rub into the flour until the mixture resembles fine breadcrumbs.

3. Add the water and mix until a ball of dough is formed.

4. Roll out to line a 8 inch pie or quiche dish.

5. Prick the bottom lightly with a fork and bake blind at 350°F for 15 minutes.

6. Remove from the oven.

7. Meanwhile, melt the butter or margarine in a frying pan and sauté the onion and pepper until just softened.

8. Arrange the onion and pepper on the bottom of the dough followed by the sliced tomatoes.

9. Beat the eggs, and add the cream and seasoning.

10. Pour over the vegetables and sprinkle the cheese on top.

11. Return to the oven for 35-40 minutes until risen and golden brown on top.

TIME: Preparation takes 25 minutes, cooking takes 55 minutes.

VARIATION: For an everyday quiche, replace the cream with milk.

188

189

LENTIL MOUSSAKA

Try a taste of the Greek Islands with this classic dish.

SERVES 4-6

1¼ cups green lentils
1 large eggplant, sliced
4-5 tbsps oil
1 large onion, chopped
1 clove garlic, crushed
1 large carrot, diced
4 sticks celery, finely chopped
1-2 tsps mixed herbs
14oz can tomatoes
2 tsps shoyu sauce (Japanese soy sauce)
Black pepper
2 medium potatoes, cooked and sliced
2 large tomatoes, sliced

Sauce
4 tbsps margarine
4 tbsps brown rice flour
Scant 2 cups milk
1 large egg, separated
½ cup grated cheddar cheese
1 tsp nutmeg

1. Cook the lentils in plenty of water until soft. Drain and reserve the liquid.

2. Fry the eggplant in the oil, drain well and set aside.

3. Sauté the onion, garlic, carrot, celery and a little of the lentil stock.

4. Simmer with the lid on until just tender.

5. Add the lentils, mixed herbs and canned tomatoes. Simmer gently for 3-4 minutes.

6. Season with the shoyu and pepper.

7. Place a layer of the lentil mixture in a large casserole dish and cover with half of the eggplant slices.

8. Cover the eggplant slices with half of the potato slices and all the tomato.

9. Repeat with the remaining lentils, eggplant and potatoes.

10. To make the sauce, melt the margarine in a saucepan, remove from the heat and stir in the flour to make a roux.

11. Add the milk gradually, blending well, so that the sauce is smooth and lump free.

12. Return to the heat and stir continually until the sauce thickens.

13. Remove the pan from the heat and cool slightly. Add the egg yolk, stir in the cheese and add the nutmeg.

14. Beat the egg white until it is stiff, then carefully fold into the sauce.

15. Pour the sauce over the moussaka, covering the dish completely.

16. Bake at 350°F for about 40 minutes until the top is golden brown and puffy.

TIME: Preparation takes 45 minutes, cooking takes 1 hour 10 minutes.

FREEZING: Assemble the mixture without the sauce and freeze. Defrost, add the sauce and cook from Step 14.

SERVING IDEA: Serve with a crunchy green salad amd bread.

SPAGHETTI BOLOGNAISE

Any cooked beans can be used in this recipe.

SERVES 2-4

12oz whole-wheat spaghetti
4 tbsps olive oil
2 medium onions, chopped
1 clove garlic, crushed
14oz can tomatoes, chopped and juice
    retained
2 small carrots, diced
2 sticks celery, sliced
1½ cups mushrooms, sliced
1 small red pepper, diced
½ tsp basil
½ tsp oregano
¼ tsp nutmeg
2 tbsps tomato paste
1¼ cups stock or water
¾ cup cooked aduki beans
2 tsps soya flour
Salt and pepper
Parmesan cheese

1. Cook the spaghetti as per the instructions on the package.

2. Heat the olive oil in a large pan and cook the onions and garlic until browned.

3. Add the canned tomatoes with their juice, the carrots, celery, mushrooms, pepper, basil, oregano, nutmeg, tomato paste, and stock.

4. Stir well and simmer for about 20 minutes or until the vegetables are cooked.

5. Add the cooked beans and cook for a further 5 minutes.

6. Mix the soy flour with a little water and add to the sauce and allow to cook for 2 minutes.

7. Season to taste.

8. Drain the spaghetti and serve topped with the bolognaise sauce and a sprinkling of Parmesan cheese.

TIME: Preparation takes about 30 minutes, cooking takes 35 minutes.

COOK'S TIP: Add a tablespoon of oil to the water in which the spaghetti is cooked to prevent it from sticking together.

VEGETARIAN PAELLA

Perfect served with crusty bread and a green salad.

SERVES 4-6

4 tbsps olive oil
1 large onion, chopped
2 cloves garlic, crushed
½ tsp paprika
1½ cups long grain brown rice
3¾ cups stock
¾ cups dry white wine
14oz can tomatoes, plus juice, chopped
1 tbsp tomato paste
½ tsp tarragon
1 tsp basil
1 tsp oregano
1 red pepper, roughly chopped
1 green pepper, roughly chopped
3 sticks celery, finely chopped
3 cups mushrooms, washed and sliced
½ cup pea pods, topped and tailed and
  cut into halves
⅔ cup frozen peas
½ cup cashew nut pieces
Salt and pepper

1. Heat the oil and fry the onion and garlic until soft.

2. Add the paprika and rice and continue to cook for 4-5 minutes until the rice is transparent. Stir occasionally.

3. Add the stock, wine, tomatoes, tomato paste and herbs and simmer for 10-15 minutes.

4. Add the pepper, celery, mushrooms and pea pods and continue to cook for another 30 minutes until the rice is cooked.

5. Add the peas, cashew nuts and seasoning to taste.

6. Heat through and place on a large heated serving dish.

7. Sprinkle the parsley over the top and garnish with lemon wedges and olives.

TIME: Preparation takes 20 minutes, cooking takes 45 minutes.

COOK'S TIP: To prepare in advance, undercook slightly, add a little more stock or water and reheat. Do not add the peas until just before serving otherwise they will lose their color.

MOORS AND CHRISTIANS

*This dish, originally from Cuba, is so called
because of the use of black beans and white rice.*

SERVES 4

1 cup black beans, soaked overnight
 and cooked until soft
2 tbsps vegetable oil
1 medium onion, chopped
4 cloves garlic, crushed
1 medium green pepper, finely chopped
2 large tomatoes, skinned and finely
 chopped
1¼ cups long grain rice
Salt and pepper
Little bean cooking water if required

1. Drain the cooked beans and mash 3
tbsps to a paste with a fork, adding a little
bean cooking water if necesssary.

2. Heat the oil and fry the onion, garlic
and pepper until soft.

3. Add the tomatoes and cook for a
further 2 minutes.

4. Add the bean paste and stir.

5. Add the cooked beans and rice, and
enough water to cover.

6. Bring to the boil, cover and simmer for
20-25 minutes until the rice is *al dente.*

7. Serve hot.

TIME: Preparation takes 15 minutes. Cooking time, 1-1½ hours for the beans, 25-30
minutes for the finished dish.

SERVING IDEA: Serve with a crisp green salad and crusty bread.

VARIATION: A small can of tomatoes may be used in place of fresh ones.

PULSES, GRAINS & PASTA

Pulses (dried beans, peas and lentils) used to be considered food for the underprivileged, but in recent years their true nutritional value has been recognised and we are now lucky to a wide selection available – all of which can be used to provide a variety of cheap and nutritional dishes.

Dried beans contain protein, vitamins, minerals and fiber, and are particularly high in vitamins B1 and B2. They also contain significant amounts of calcium, phosphorous, and iron. Dried pulses should always be washed thoroughly before use and then left to stand in water for the time recommended on the packet. Once the pulses have been soaked, transfer to a saucepan and cover with fresh water. Bring to the boil and simmer for the first 10 minutes, turn down the heat and continue boiling slowly until the beans are cooked. To test, remove a bean from the pot, hold between thumb and forefinger and squeeze gently. If the bean yields to the pressure it should be soft enough to eat.

Grains are another important food group. These botanic grasses are the staple food of most of the world, and are the cheapest most important source of energy. A wide variety of grains are available, but the majority of people still tend to use only a small proportion of them, such as pearl barley, oats and rice. There are many other delicious grains to choose from. Millet, for instance, can be made into a breakfast dish, bulgar salad makes a nice change from rice salad, and buckwheat is excellent in casseroles and roasts.

Home-made pasta is a delight and far superior to most shop-bought relatives. This chapter includes two recipes for fresh pasta which you can incorporate into your repertoire, and once you've made your own pasta you'll never want to buy it again.

BOULANGERE VEGETABLE BAKE

*Named after the classic French potato dish that was
traditionally cooked in the village baker's oven.*

SERVES 4

½ cup black beans, soaked overnight and
   cooked until tender
1 medium cauliflower, divided into
   florets
3½ cups water
1 bay leaf
1¼ cups milk
2 tbsps sunflower oil
1 medium onion, very finely chopped
⅓ cup fine whole-wheat flour
1 tbsp wholegrain mustard
1 tbsp parsley, chopped
Salt and pepper
3 medium potatoes, cooked and cut
   ¼ inch slices
2 tbsps butter or margarine

1. Wash and drain the cauliflower florets.

2. Bring the water to the boil in a large
pan, add the bay leaf and a little salt.

3. Plunge the cauliflower into the water,
return to the boil, cover and poach the
florets for 8-10 minutes until just cooked.

4. Drain, discard the bay leaf and reserve
the cooking water.

5. Mix the milk with enough cooking

water to make 2½ cups.

6. Heat the oil in a small pan and gently
sauté the onion until soft.

7. Stir in the flour and cook over a gentle
heat for 1-2 minutes.

8. Gradually add the milk and water,
stirring all the time to avoid lumps.

9. Add the mustard and cook gently for a
further 3 minutes.

10. Drain the cooked beans and return
them to a large pan, add the cauliflower
and mix well.

11. Pour the mustard sauce over the beans
and cauliflower and stir in the chopped
parsley and seasoning.

12. Place the mixture in a greased
3¾ cups casserole dish.

13. Top with the sliced potatoes,
overlapping them slightly, and dot with
the butter or margarine.

14. Bake at 350°F for 20-25 minutes until
the top is nicely browned.

TIME: Preparation takes 25 minutes.

Cooking time, including the beans, 1 hour 10 minutes.

FREEZING: Freeze the base for 4-6 weeks and add the topping when required.

COOK'S TIP: Adding a bay leaf to the water when cooking cauliflower
eliminates the strong smell.

VEGETARIAN SHEPHERD'S PIE

*This pie will serve 2 people without
any accompaniments and 4 people if served with vegetables.*

SERVES 2-4

½ cup brown lentils
¼ cup pot barley
Scant 2 cups stock or water
1 tsp yeast extract
1 large carrot, diced
½ onion, chopped finely
1 clove garlic, crushed
½ cup walnuts, roughly chopped
1 tsp vegetarian gravy powder or
    thickener
Salt and pepper
3 medium potatoes, cooked and mashed

1. Simmer the lentils and barley in 1¼ cups of the stock and yeast extract for 30 minutes.

2. Meanwhile, cook the carrot, onion, garlic and walnuts in the remaining stock for 15 minutes or until tender.

3. Mix the gravy powder or thickener with a little water and add to the carrot mixture, stir over a low heat until thickened.

4. Combine the lentils and barley with the carrot mixture, season and place in an ovenproof dish.

5. Cover with the mashed potato and cook at 350°F for about 30 minutes until browned on top.

TIME: Preparation takes 15 minutes, cooking takes 1 hour.

SERVING IDEA: Garnish with broiled tomatoes and serve with vegetables in season, broccoli, sprouts, cabbage etc.

BUCKWHEAT SAVORY

*Garnish this tasty recipe with fronds of fennel
and serve with a fennel and orange salad.*

SERVES 4

1 tbsp raisins
1 medium onion, finely chopped
1-2 cloves garlic, crushed
2 sticks celery, finely chopped
Oil
1-2 tsps garam masala
¼ tsp ground cumin
1 cup buckwheat
2 medium carrots, diced
1 small red pepper, diced
¾ cup cashew nuts, roughly chopped
2 tsps tomato paste
1 tsp yeast extract or bouillon powder
    dissolved in 1 cup boiling water
Salt and pepper
2 zucchini, cut into bite-sized pieces

1. Soak the sultanas in a little water for
about 1 hour.

2. Place the onion, garlic and celery in a
saucepan with a little oil and sauté
together for about 4 minutes.

3. Add the garam masala and cumin and
cook for a further minute.

4. Add the remaining ingredients, except
the raisins and zucchini.

5. Simmer for about 20 minutes or until
the buckwheat is soft and chewy but do
not allow the mixture to become too dry.

6. Add the raisins and zucchini and cook
for a further 5 minutes. The zucchini
should not be allowed to become too soft.

7. Transfer to a heated serving dish and
serve at once.

TIME: Preparation takes 15 minutes, soaking takes 1 hour and cooking takes 30 minutes.

VARIATION: Any leftover mixture can be used as a stuffing for peppers. Bake the
peppers for about 20 minutes, fill and place in a covered dish. Bake for a
further 10 minutes until piping hot.

BULGAR RISOTTO

*This makes a quick lunch dish and is
particularly handy if unexpected guests call.*

SERVES 3-4

1 cup bulgar wheat
1 medium onion, peeled and finely
    chopped
2 sticks celery, finely chopped
1-2 cloves garlic, crushed
1 tbsp butter
1 small red pepper, diced
1 small green pepper, diced
½ tsp dried mixed herbs
½ cup peanuts, chopped
1 tsp vegetable extract or bouillon powder
    dissolved in ¼ cup boiling water
2 tsps shoyu sauce (Japanese soy sauce)
½ cup corn
½ cup peas
Salt and pepper
Juice of half a lemon

1. Put the bulgar wheat into a bowl and
cover with boiling water.

2. Leave for about 10 minutes after which
time the water will have been absorbed
and the wheat swollen.

3. Meanwhile, place the onion, celery and
garlic into a saucepan and sauté for a few
minutes in the butter.

4. Add the peppers, herbs, nuts and
vegetable extract.

5. Simmer over a low heat for about 8
minutes.

6. Add the bulgar wheat, shoyu, corn,
peas and seasoning and mix together well.

7. Continue cooking for a further 5
minutes.

8. Mix in the lemon juice and transfer to a
heated serving dish.

9. Serve immediately.

TIME: Preparation takes 15 minutes, cooking takes 20 minutes.

SERVING IDEA: Serve with a crisp green salad.

WATCHPOINT: If the risotto is too dry, add a little more water or stock.

MILLET CROQUETTES WITH YOGURT SAUCE

*Croquettes are always popular and yogurt
sauce makes these even more tempting!*

MAKES ABOUT 15

1 medium onion, peeled and finely
   chopped
1 clove garlic, crushed
1 tsp dried mixed herbs or 2 tbsps freshly
   chopped parsley
Oil
1 cup millet flakes
1¼-2 cups water
1 tbsp tomato paste
1 tsp vegetable extract (optional)
¾ cup cheddar cheese, grated
¼ tsp paprika
Salt and pepper
Whole-wheat breadcrumbs

Sauce
1¼ cups thick set plain yogurt
2 tbsps freshly chopped parsley
Salt and pepper
Pinch of paprika
A little lemon juice (optional)

1. Sauté the onion, garlic and mixed herbs in a little oil until soft.

2. Place the millet flakes in a separate pan with the water, bring to the boil and simmer gently, stirring constantly until a thick texture results.

3. Cool a little.

4. Add the remaining croquette ingredients, except the breadcrumbs, and mix together well.

5. Shape into cakes and coat with the crumbs.

6. Fry in very shallow oil on both sides until crisp and golden.

7. To make the sauce, mix all the ingredients together well.

TIME: Preparation takes 15 minutes, cooking takes 15 minutes.

SERVING IDEA: Serve with the sauce handed round separately.

VARIATION: Vary the flavor by using freshly chopped mint instead of the mixed herbs or parsley. Fresh basil also makes a delicious alternative.

MILLET MEDLEY

A tasty and wholesome recipe for the whole family.

SERVES 4

1 medium onion, chopped
2 tbsps oil
1 cup millet
2½ cups stock or water
Salt and pepper
½ cup cooked peas
½ cup corn
4 sticks celery, chopped
½ cup sunflower seeds
2 tbsps shoyu sauce (Japanese soy sauce)

1. Sauté the onion in the oil for 2-3 minutes.

2. Add the dry millet and cook for a few minutes, stirring all the time.

3. Add the stock and seasoning, bring to the boil and simmer over a low heat for 30 minutes.

4. Allow to cool.

5. Add the peas, corn and celery and mix well.

6. Place the sunflower seeds and shoyu into a frying pan and cook over a medium heat, stirring continuously until the seeds are dry. Cool.

7. Just before serving, sprinkle with the toasted sunflower seeds.

TIME: Preparation takes 10 minutes, cooking takes 40 minutes.

SERVING IDEA: Serve garnished with tomatoes.

VARIATION: Replace the sunflower seeds with pumpkin seeds.

PEANUT RISOTTO

A crunchy textured dish to serve on the side or as a main course.

SERVES 4

1 large onion, chopped
1 clove garlic, crushed
1 tbsp vegetable oil
¾ cup short grain brown rice
1 cup peanuts, roughly chopped
1½ cups mushrooms, sliced
2½ cups boiling water
¾ cup green beans
¼ cup raisins
2 tsps dried oregano
2 tsps lemon juice
Salt and pepper

1. Fry the onion and garlic in the oil for 3-4 minutes.

2. Add the rice and peanuts to toast for 1-2 minutes.

3. Add the mushrooms and cook for a further 3-4 minutes, then add the boiling water, stir once and simmer for 30 minutes.

4. Add the beans, raisins, herbs, lemon juice and seasoning and cook for a further 5-10 minutes.

TIME: Preparation takes 10 minutes, cooking takes 50 minutes.

SERVING IDEA: Serve garnished with lemon wedges and parsley.

VARIATION: Use this mixture to stuff cabbage, spinach or vine leaves.

Savory Grain Casserole

*Serve as a complete meal for 2 people or serve
accompanied with lightly steamed vegetables for 4 people*

SERVES 2-4

½ cup brown rice
½ cup split peas
2 sticks celery, very finely chopped
1 medium onion, very finely chopped
1½ cups mushrooms, chopped
14oz can tomatoes, drained and chopped
  or tomatoes, peeled and chopped
½ tsp dill seeds
½ tsp thyme
2 tbsps shoyu sauce (Japanese soy sauce)
1 egg, beaten
1 cup cheddar cheese, grated

1. Cover the rice with water and cook for
10-15 minutes; drain.

2. Cover the split peas with water and
cook for 20 minutes until just tender but
not mushy; drain.

3. Meanwhile, combine the celery, onion,
mushrooms, tomatoes, dill, thyme, shoyu
and the egg in a large bowl.

4. Stir in the rice and peas.

5. Place the mixture in a greased
ovenproof casserole dish and cook for 45
minutes at 350°F.

6. Remove from the oven and sprinkle
with the grated cheese.

7. Return to the oven for 10 minutes until
the cheese has melted.

8. Serve at once.

TIME: Preparation takes 10 minutes, cooking takes 1 hour 45 minutes.

SERVING IDEA: Garnish with a few whole cooked mushrooms or broiled tomatoes.

WHOLE-WHEAT PASTA

Home-made pasta is always superior to the shop-bought varieties.

MAKES 1lb

2½ cups whole-wheat flour
Large pinch of salt
3 eggs
1 tbsp olive oil

---

1. Put the flour and salt into a large mixing bowl or heap on a pastry board, make a well in the center and break in the eggs and add the olive oil.

2. Mix together with a fork until the dough can be gathered into a rough ball. If the dough is too dry and will not come together, add a few drops of water.

3. Knead the dough well for 5-10 minutes, incorporating all the flour left on the board, until it is smooth, shiny and no longer sticky.

4. Cover the dough with plastic wrap and leave to rest in a cool place for half an hour.

5. Divide the dough into two, wrapping one half in plastic wrap to stop it drying out.

6. Lightly flour the working surface and rolling pin and roll out the dough as thinly as possible, turning and dusting with flour underneath as for pastry. The pasta should be thin enough to be able to see the shadow of a hand against it when held up to the light.

TIME: Preparation takes 20 minutes.

FREEZING: Freeze for up to three months. De-frost and use as for fresh pasta.

SPINACH PASTA

*This tasty and colorful pasta can be used
in numerous Italian dishes.*

MAKES 1lb

2½ cups plain whole-wheat flour
Large pinch of salt
2 eggs
½ cup cooked spinach, finely chopped
1 tbsp olive oil

1. Put the flour and salt into a large mixing bowl or heap on a pastry board, and make a well in the center.

2. Mix the eggs with the spinach and pour this into the center of the flour along with the olive oil.

3. Mix together with a fork until the dough can be gathered into a rough ball.

4. Add a little water or extra oil if the dough is a little dry.

5. Roll out in the same way as whole wheat pasta and use as you would pre-packed pasta.

TIME: Preparation takes 20 minutes.

FREEZING: Freeze for up to three months. De-frost and use as for fresh pasta.

VARIATIONS: Tomato Pasta – Replace one of the eggs with 3 tbsps of tomato paste for a delicate pink-colored pasta.
Saffron Pasta – Use two eggs plus two egg yolks and 1 tsp saffron powder. This gives a golden color which will show better if the whole-wheat flour is replaced with unbleached plain flour in the same quantity.

SPICY BLACK-EYED PEAS

A spicy dish from the West Indies.

SERVES 4

2 cups black-eyed peas, soaked and cooked
4 tbsps vegetable oil
1 large onion, finely chopped
2 cloves garlic, crushed
1 tsp ground cinnamon
½ tsp ground cumin
Salt and pepper
⅔ cup bean liquid or water
2 tbsps tomato paste
1 tbsp shoyu sauce (Japanese soy sauce)
2 large tomatoes, skinned and chopped
1 tbsp chopped parsley

1. Drain the beans well and retain the cooking liquid.

2. Heat the oil and fry the onion and garlic for 4-5 minutes until soft.

3. Stir in the cinnamon, cumin and seasoning and cook for a further 2 minutes.

4. Add the beans, bean stock, tomato paste, shoyu sauce and tomatoes.

5. Stir and bring to the boil.

6. Simmer for 15-20 minutes until thick.

7. Check the seasoning.

8. Serve poured over cooked pasta and sprinkled with chopped parsley.

TIME: Preparation takes 20 minutes. Cooking time, including the beans, 1 hour 35 minutes.

SERVING IDEA: Serve over cooked rice and garnish with lemon wedges.

VARIATION: Navy beans can be used in place of black-eyed peas.

BUTTER BEAN AND SPINACH ROLL WITH LEMON CRUST

The lemon crust gives just the right edge of flavor to make the whole dish a little bit special.

SERVES 4

1 cup butter beans, soaked overnight and cooked until tender
1 cup fresh spinach
½ tsp freshly grated nutmeg
Salt and freshly ground black pepper
½ cup cheddar cheese, grated
1 egg, beaten
1 tsp sunflower oil
½ cup fresh breadcrumbs
1 tbsp sesame seeds
Grated rind of 1 lemon
2 tsps lemon juice

1. Preheat the oven to 400°F.

2. Drain the cooked beans, transfer to a large bowl and mash well.

3. Wash and trim the spinach. Using a pan with a close fitting lid, cook the spinach, with no added water, for 5 minutes.

4. When cooked and cool enough to handle, chop the spinach finely and add the nutmeg and seasoning.

5. Stir the grated cheese and beaten egg into the mashed butterbeans.

6. Place a sheet of plastic wrap on the work surface and spread the bean mixture over it in a rectangle measuring roughly 7 x 11 inch.

7. Cover the bean layer with the chopped spinach.

8. With the short end towards you, lift the edge of the plastic wrap and gently roll the mixture into a cylinder, using the wrap to support the roll.

9. In a bowl, rub the oil into the breadcrumbs and stir in the sesame seeds and lemon rind.

10. Spread the breadcrumb mixture over the working surface and roll the butter bean roll over it until it is well covered.

11. Transfer the roll to a greased cookie sheet, sprinkle with the lemon juice and bake for 15-20 minutes until the crust is crisp and golden.

TIME: Preparation takes 15 minutes. Cooking time, including the beans, 1 hour 30 minutes.

SERVING IDEA: Serve with a colorful mixed pepper salad.

BUTTER BEANS AND MUSHROOMS AU GRATIN

*You can vary the flavor of this dish by
substituting other kinds of beans.*

SERVES 4

¾ cup butter beans, soaked overnight and
    cooked until soft
⅓ cup butter
1 tbsp lemon juice
Salt and pepper
3 cups mushrooms, separate the caps
    from the stalks
¼ cup whole-wheat breadcrumbs
¼ cup grated cheese

Sauce
4 tbsps margarine
4 tbsps flour
1¼ cups milk

1. Mix the beans with 4 tbsps of the
butter, lemon juice and salt and pepper.

2. Place the mixture in the bottom of a pie
dish.

3. Melt the remaining butter in a pan and
fry the mushroom caps for about 5
minutes.

4. Make the sauce by melting the
margarine and stirring in the flour, cook
for about 2 minutes and then gradually
add the milk, stirring all the time until the
sauce thickens.

5. Chop the mushroom stalks and add to
the sauce, pour this over the beans.

6. Place the cooked mushroom caps,
underside upwards, on the top and
sprinkle with the breadcrumbs and
cheese.

7. Bake in a moderate oven, 375°F, for
about 15 minutes until the top is brown.

TIME: Preparation takes 15 minutes, cooking takes 35 minutes.

SERVING IDEA: Serve with lightly steamed green vegetables.

CHICKPEA STEW

You can use canned chickpeas (garbanzo beans) for this recipe but the dried ones have a much nicer flavor.

SERVES 4

1 large onion, finely chopped
1 large carrot, diced
1 tbsp vegetable oil
2 large potatoes, peeled and diced
14oz can of tomatoes
1 tsp dried basil
Freshly ground black pepper
2 cups cooked chickpeas

1. Place the onion, carrot and oil in a pan and fry gently for about 5 minutes.

2. Add the potatoes, tomatoes and their juice, herbs and pepper.

3. Cover and simmer gently for about 30 minutes or until the potatoes are soft. Stir occasionally to make sure that the potatoes do not stick to the bottom of the pan.

4. Add the cooked chickpeas and warm through gently.

TIME: Preparation takes about 20 minutes, cooking takes 35-40 minutes.

SERVING IDEA: Serve with cooked green vegetables such as broccoli, peas or cabbage.

Chana Masala

*An excellent dish to serve hot as a main course or cold
as an accompaniment to a nut loaf.*

SERVES 4

1 large onion, chopped
4 cloves garlic, crushed
¾ inch piece of fresh ginger, peeled and
    finely chopped
3 tbsps margarine
1 tbsp ground coriander
2 tsps cumin seed
¼ tsp cayenne pepper
1 tsp turmeric
2 tsps roasted cumin seed, ground
1 tbsp lemon juice
2 tsps paprika
14oz can plum tomatoes
3 cups cooked chickpeas
1 tsp garam masala
½ tsp salt
1 fresh green chili pepper, finely chopped

1. Sauté the onion, garlic and ginger in the margarine until soft.

2. Add all the spices and lemon juice and fry over a low heat for 1-2 minutes stirring all the time.

3. Add the tomatoes, roughly chopped, together with their juice.

4. Add the cooked chickpeas.

5. Cook for 30 minutes over a medium heat.

6. Add the garam masala, salt and chili pepper, stir well and serve.

TIME: Preparation takes about 15 minutes, cooking takes 30 minutes.

SERVING IDEA: Serve hot with coconut rice and mango chutney. This dish improves with time and is always more flavorful the following day.

WATCHPOINT: Fry the spices over a low heat to ensure they do not burn.

VARIATION: Small pieces of diced vegetables such as potatoes, fresh tomatoes or cauliflower may be added.

CHICKPEA BURGERS

These burgers are nice cold and are
useful for a packed lunch or picnic.

SERVES 4

2½ cups cooked chickpeas or 2 x 14oz
   cans chickpeas
1 onion, finely chopped
2 cloves garlic, crushed
2 medium potatoes, cooked and mashed
2 tbsps shoyu sauce (Japanese soy sauce)
2 tsps lemon juice
Black pepper
Whole-wheat flour
Oil for frying

1. Put the chickpeas into a large bowl and mash well.

2. Add the onion, garlic, potato, shoyu, lemon juice and pepper. Mix together well.

3. With floured hands, shape heaped tablespoonfuls of the mixture into small burgers.

4. Coat each burger with flour and refrigerate for 1 hour.

5. Heat a little oil and gently fry the burgers on each side until golden brown.

TIME: Preparation takes 15 minutes, cooking takes about 15 minutes.

SERVING IDEA: Serve with a hot, spicy tomato sauce.

FREEZING: Cook and freeze for up to 2 months.

CHESTNUT HOT-POT

This enticing hot-pot is perfect served with a lightly cooked green vegetable.

SERVES 4-6

4 medium potatoes
3 medium onions
1 cup brown lentils
2 cups chestnuts
Salt and pepper
2 tsps yeast extract (optional)
Scant 2 cups warm water
4 tbsps margarine

1. Peel and slice the potatoes and onions thinly.

2. Put layers of potatoes, onions, lentils and chestnuts into a greased pie dish ending with a layer of potatoes. Season well between each layer.

3. If using, dissolve the yeast extract in the warm water and pour over.

4. Dot with margarine and cover.

5. Bake at 375°F for an hour or until the potatoes are tender.

6. Turn up the oven to 400°F, remove the lid from the casserole and return to the oven for 10-15 minutes until the potatoes are crispy and golden brown.

TIME: Preparation takes 20 minutes, cooking takes 1 hour 15 minutes.

VARIATION: Dried chestnuts may be used but need to be soaked overnight in stock or water. Canned chestnuts work well, too. Add bouillon powder to the water instead of yeast extract.

GREEN LENTILS WITH FRESH GINGER AND SPICES

There's certainly no lack of taste in this spicy lentil mix.

SERVES 4

¾ cup green or Continental lentils

Water or stock to cover

2 tbsps margarine or 1 tbsp soya or sunflower oil

1 medium onion, peeled and finely chopped

1 inch piece fresh root ginger, peeled and grated or finely chopped

1 tsp garam masala

1 tsp cumin seeds

1 tsp coriander seeds, crushed

1 tsp green cardamom pods, seeds removed and crushed

1 medium carrot, scrubbed and diced

14oz can peeled Italian tomatoes

¾ cup mushrooms, cleaned and finely chopped

1 tbsp shoyu sauce (Japanese soy sauce)

1 tbsp cider vinegar

Salt and freshly ground black pepper to taste

Freshly chopped parsley or coriander to garnish

1. Pick over the lentils and wash thoroughly.

2. Place in a large, thick-bottomed saucepan, cover with water or stock and bring to the boil. Turn off the heat, cover and leave to begin to swell.

3. Meanwhile, heat the margarine or oil in a separate saucepan and gently fry the onion, ginger and spices until they are well combined, softening and giving off a tempting aroma.

4. Add to the lentils, bring to the boil and start to add the other vegetables, allowing several minutes between each addition, beginning with the carrot followed by the tomatoes and lastly the chopped mushrooms.

5. Stir frequently to prevent sticking and check on liquid quantity regularly, adding more water or stock as necessary.

6. Just before the end of the cooking time – approximately 25 minutes depending on the age of the lentils – add the shoyu, cider vinegar and salt and pepper.

7. Cook for a few more minutes and serve hot garnished with slices of lemon and freshly chopped parsley or coriander.

TIME: Preparation takes about 25 minutes, cooking takes about 45 minutes.

SERVING IDEA: Serve with boiled wholegrain rice or baked potatoes and salad made from beansprouts, red and green peppers and grated daikon.

VARIATION: Black olives can replace the chopped parsley or coriander.

LENTIL SAVORY

This dish is quick and easy to prepare and very nutritious.

SERVES 4

¾ cup lentils
½ tsp basil
½ tsp mixed herbs
2 medium onions, chopped
4 tbsps margarine
2 tbsps tomato paste
14oz can tomatoes
1 tsp brown sugar
Salt and black pepper
⅔ cup sour cream
1½ cups sliced cheddar cheese

1. Soak the lentils overnight.

2. Add the herbs and simmer with the lentils in the cooking water until tender.

3. Sauté the onion in the fat until soft. Add the lentils and all the other ingredients apart from cheese and cream.

4. Simmer for 15 minutes until thickened and pour into a greased ovenproof dish.

5. Cover with the cream and cheese and broil or bake at 375°F until the cheese has melted.

TIME: Preparation takes 15 minutes, cooking takes 35-45 minutes.

COOK'S TIP: The sour cream can be served separately if desired.

SERVING IDEA: Serve hot with a mixed salad.

FREEZING: This lentil savoury will freeze well but do not cover it with cream and cheese until you are reheating it.

PIPER'S PIE

Accompany this attractive dish with carrots
and corn for the perfect family meal.

SERVES 4

3 medium potatoes, peeled and diced
¾ cup mung beans
2 leeks
2 carrots
½ tsp dill
1 inch fresh ginger, chopped or finely
  grated
1 tbsp concentrated apple juice
1 tsp miso

1. Boil the potatoes and mash with a little butter and seasoning.

2. In a separate pan, cover the mung beans with water and boil for 15-20 minutes until soft.

3. Meanwhile, generously butter an ovenproof casserole dish and put in the leeks, carrots, dill, ginger and concentrated apple juice. Mix well.

4. Drain the beans, reserving the stock, and add to the casserole dish.

5. Dissolve the miso in a little of the bean stock and mix into the casserole which should be moist but not too wet.

6. Cover and cook at 400°F for 30-45 minutes, stirring a couple of times during the cooking and adding a little more bean stock if necessary.

7. Remove from the oven and cover with a layer of mashed potatoes.

8. Return to the oven to brown or brown under the broiler.

TIME: Preparation takes 20 minutes, cooking takes 50-60 minutes.

VARIATION: A small can of corn may be added to the pie before covering with the mashed potatoes.

238

RED BEAN STEW WITH CHILI SAUCE

For convenience and speed canned kidney beans can be used in this recipe.

SERVES 4

¾ cup dried red kidney beans, soaked overnight
2 tbsps oil
1 large onion, chopped
1 clove garlic, crushed
14oz can tomatoes
½ tsp dried oregano
½ tsp dried basil
½ tsp shoyu sauce (Japanese soy sauce)
3 medium potatoes, peeled and diced
Salt and pepper

Chili Sauce
2 tbsps butter or margarine
1 small clove garlic, crushed
1 small onion, grated
¾ tsp chili powder
1 tbsp cider vinegar
⅓ cup bean stock or water
A little salt
1 tsp tomato paste
1 tbsp fresh coriander, finely chopped
1 tsp plain yogurt

1. Drain the beans, put into a large pan and cover with water. Boil vigorously for 10-15 minutes, turn down the heat and cook for about an hour until the beans are tender but still whole.

2. Heat the oil and fry the onion and garlic until soft.

3. Add the tomatoes, oregano, basil, shoyu and potatoes, cover and cook for 20 minutes until the potatoes are softened. Season to taste.

4. Drain the beans, reserving a little stock, and add to the onion and tomato mixture.

5. Cook gently for 5-10 minutes.

6. In a separate pan, melt the butter or margarine and cook the garlic and onion until soft.

7. Add the chili powder and cook for a further 1-2 minutes.

8. Add the vinegar, stock, salt, tomato paste and coriander and cook for 5 minutes.

9. Remove from the heat and leave to cool slightly before stirring in the yogurt.

10. Serve with the sauce handed round separately.

TIME: Preparation takes 20 minutes. Cooking time, including the beans, 1 hour 35 minutes.

241

BEANY LASAGNE

*This tasty lasagne is suitable for a family
meal or entertaining friends.*

SERVES 4-6

8 strips whole-wheat lasagne
1 large onion, peeled and finely chopped
1 tbsp vegetable oil
1-2 cloves garlic, crushed
1 cup cooked aduki beans
1 green pepper, de-seeded and chopped
14oz can chopped tomatoes
1 tbsp tomato paste
1 tsp dried basil
1 tsp dried oregano
Shoyu sauce (Japanese soy sauce) or salt
Freshly ground black pepper

Sauce
2 tbsps margarine or butter
2 tbsps plain whole-wheat flour
Scant 2 cups dairy or soy milk
½ cup cheddar cheese, grated (optional)
Salt
Freshly ground black pepper

1. Cook the lasagne in a large pan of boiling, salted water for 8-10 minutes until "al-dente". Drain well and drape over a cooling rack or the sides of a colander to cool and prevent sticking together.

2. Soften the onion in a little oil, sprinkling with a little salt to draw out the juice. Add the crushed garlic.

3. Add the beans, green pepper, chopped tomatoes, tomato paste and herbs.

4. Simmer for about 10 minutes or until the vegetables are tender.

5. Add shoyu sauce and season to taste.

6. To make the sauce, combine the margarine, flour and cold milk. Gradually bring to the boil, stirring continuously.

7. When thickened, allow to simmer, partly covered, for approximately 6 minutes.

8. Stir the cheese into the sauce and season.

9. Layer the lasagne in a greased dish in the following order: half the bean mix, half the pasta, rest of the bean mix, rest of the pasta, and top with the cheese sauce.

10. Bake at 350°F for 35 minutes or until golden brown and bubbling.

11. Serve in the dish in which it has been cooked.

TIME: Preparation takes 20 minutes, cooking takes about 60 minutes.

SERVING IDEA: Serve with a green salad.

COOK'S TIP: Pre-cooked lasagne can be used but it is important to add an extra amount of liquid to the dish in order to allow the pasta to absorb enough fluid while cooking.

SWEET BEAN CURRY

This excellent curry will freeze well for up to six weeks.

SERVES 4

¾ cup red kidney beans, soaked
   overnight
2 tbsps butter or margarine
1 onion, sliced
1 apple, cored and chopped
2 cups mushrooms, sliced
1 tbsp curry powder
2 tbsps unbleached flour
2½ cups bean stock or bean stock
   and water
Salt to taste
1 tbsp lemon juice
1 tbsp chutney
½ cup raisins
½ cup coconut flaked

---

1. Drain the beans, put into a large pan and cover with cold water.

2. Bring to the boil and boil vigorously for 10-15 minutes, turn down the heat and boil for about an hour until the beans are tender but still whole.

3. Melt the butter or margarine and cook the onion until it is very brown.

4. Add the apple and mushrooms and cook for 2-3 minutes.

5. Add the curry powder and flour and cook for a couple of minutes, stirring all the time.

6. Gradually add the bean stock and stir until smooth.

7. Add the seasoning, lemon juice, chutney, raisins and beans and cook for 10-15 minutes.

8. Just before serving add the coconut and stir until softened.

TIME: Preparation takes 25 minutes. Cooking time, including the beans, 1 hour 25 minutes.

SERVING IDEA: Serve with boiled brown rice and fried plantains – peel, cut into slices and fry in hot oil until golden brown. If unavailable you can use unripe green bananas. Garnish the curry with quarters of hard-cooked eggs.

MUESLI DE-LUXE

*Dried mixed fruit and organic muesli base can
be purchased at most healthfood stores
or you can mix your own if preferred.*

MAKES 3½ lbs

4 cups mixed fruit (apples, pears,
   apricots, prunes)
2½ cups organic mueslie base
   (wheatflakes, oats, rye flakes,
   pearl barley flakes, jumbo oat flakes)
½ cup wheatgerm
1 cup sunflower seeds
1½ cups golden raisins
1½ cups raisins
1 cup hazel nuts
1 cup brazil nuts, halved

1. Chop the dried mixed fruit into small pieces with a pair of kitchen scissors.

2. Place in a mixing bowl with all the other ingredients.

3. Mix well.

4. Store in an airtight container in a cool place.

TIME: Preparation takes 10 minutes.

SERVING IDEA: Serve for breakfast with milk, soy milk, yogurt or fruit juice and add fresh fruit whenever possible or simmer with milk, water or fruit juice for 5 minutes and eat hot. Muesli can be used as a base for cookies and a topping for fruit crisps.

VARIATION: The nuts can be varied according to taste and pumpkin seeds can be added.

GRANOLA

Serve for breakfast with milk, soy milk, fruit juices or yogurt.

MAKES 1.5KG/3¼ lbs

2½ cups organic muesli base
   (wheatflakes, porridge oats, rye flakes,
   pearl barley flakes, jumbo oat flakes)
1 cup sunflower seeds
½ cup wheatgerm
1 cup sesame seeds
¾ cup soy flour
4 tbsps dried skimmed milk powder
½ cup flaked coconut
1 cup chopped mixed nuts
¾ cup sunflower or safflower oil
¾ cup clear honey
1½ cups raisins

1. Put all the ingredients apart from the raisins into a large mixing bowl.

2. Stir with a wooden spoon until all the dry ingredients are coated with the oil and honey.

3. Spread the mixture evenly over 2 large cookie sheets.

4. Bake at 300°F for about 1 hour stirring frequently until the mixture is golden brown.

5. Remove from the oven and allow to cool on the trays.

6. Add the raisins and mix well.

7. Place in an airtight container and store in a cool place.

TIME: Preparation takes 10 minutes, cooking takes 1 hour.

COOK'S TIP: Organic muesli base and chopped mixed nuts can be purchased at most health food stores.

VARIATION: To vary the flavor, use molasses in place of honey – this may need to be heated slightly before incorporating it into the Granola.

BUTTER BEAN ONE-POT

This is a quick to make, all-in-one supper dish.

SERVES 4

2 tbsps vegetable oil
1 green pepper, finely chopped
1 large onion, finely chopped
2 sticks celery, diced
14oz can tomatoes
2 large potatoes, peeled and diced
1¼ cups vegetable stock or water
2 tbsps finely chopped parsley
Salt and pepper
2 cups cooked butter beans

1. Put the oil, pepper, onion and celery into a pan and cook gently until the onion begins to brown.

2. Add the tomatoes and their juice, plus the potatoes, stock, parsley, salt and pepper.

3. Simmer for about 30 minutes or until the liquid is reduced by half.

4. Add the beans and heat through gently for 5-10 minutes.

TIME: Preparation takes about 15 minutes, cooking takes 50 minutes.

SERVING IDEA: Serve with lots of crusty bread. Garlic bread also goes well with this dish.

BUTTER BEANS IN TOMATO SAUCE

*A tasty tomato sauce perfectly complements
the beans in this easy recipe.*

SERVES 4-6

¾ cup butter beans, soaked overnight
4 tbsps vegetable shortening
1 onion, sliced
6 medium tomatoes, sliced
4 tbsps flour
1 bay leaf
A little milk
Salt and pepper
Chopped parsley

1. Drain the butter beans and put into a pan with fresh water to cover, and cook slowly until soft.

2. Melt the shortening and cook the onions with the tomatoes and bay leaf until soft.

3. Stir in the flour, and add a little cooking water from the beans to make a thick sauce.

4. Stir well and add a little milk and seasoning to taste.

5. Remove the bay leaf and pour the sauce over the beans.

6. Sprinkle with the chopped parsley.

TIME: Preparation takes 20 minutes. Cooking time, including the beans, 1½ -1¾ hours.

SERVING IDEA: Serve with baked potatoes and lightly cooked vegetables.

COOK'S TIP: When cold, mash to make a sandwich paste or use with a mixed salad. Any leftovers can be used as a basis for soup.

COOKING FOR SPECIAL OCCASIONS

How often have you heard the phrase "Oh, it's nothing, I just threw it together at the last minute"? There are, however, few people who can say this in all truth. For the most part, a good host or hostess will have spent half the time on the planning, one quarter of the time shopping and the remaining time actually cooking the meal. From a picnic to a dinner party, a barbecue to a buffet, the secret is forward planning.

Make lists – they are invaluable, not only for shopping, but for all the steps you must take to the big event. There is nothing more frustrating than to be serving the appetizer only to realise you haven't put the vegetables on to cook. When selecting your menu, try to choose some dishes that can be prepared in advance. You owe it to yourself to enjoy the occasion and your guests will not expect you to be slaving away in the kitchen for long periods before and during the meal. If you are not very experienced, try to choose two courses that do not require last minute attention: a pre-prepared soup and a cold dessert will give plenty of time to concentrate on the main course.

This chapter features a variety of dishes that are appropriate for occasions such as dinner parties, intimate meals and Christmas dinner. So no matter what the event you'll never again have to worry about what to serve your vegetarian guests.

CELERY STUFFED WITH SMOKED TOFU PATÉ

These tasty nibbles are perfect for parties, picnics and buffets.

---

4 tbsps hard vegetarian margarine
1 medium onion, chopped
1 clove garlic, chopped
½ bunch watercress, roughly chopped
¾ cup smoked tofu
½ cup cheddar cheese, grated
1 head celery
A little paprika

---

1. Melt the margarine and fry the onion and garlic until soft.

2. Add the watercress and stir for 15 seconds until it becomes limp.

3. Place in a food processor with the rest of the ingredients, excluding the celery and paprika.

4. Process until smooth, pushing down with a wooden spoon if necessary.

5. Leave to cool.

6. Clean the celery, stuff with the paté and sprinkle with a little paprika.

7. Refrigerate for at least 2 hours before serving.

TIME: Preparation and cooking takes about 15 minutes.

VARIATION: Serve with twist of lemon and very thin brown bread and butter.

FREEZING: This paté freezes well for up to 6 weeks. Thaw at room temperature for 2 hours or overnight in the refrigerator.

BRAZILIAN AVOCADOS

*The perfect way to impress your dinner guests
right from the first course.*

SERVES 4

2 large ripe avocados
A little lemon juice
Salt and pepper
½ cup finely chopped Brazil nuts
½ cup cheddar cheese, grated
2 tbsps Parmesan cheese
2 level tbsps freshly chopped parsley
2 firm ripe tomatoes, skinned and finely
   chopped
Whole-wheat breadcrumbs
2 tbsps melted butter
A little paprika

1. Halve the avocados and carefully remove the flesh from the skins. Brush the inside of the skins with a little of the lemon juice.

2. Dice the avocado and put into a bowl with a sprinkling of lemon juice and the seasoning.

3. Add the nuts, cheeses, parsley and tomato.

4. Mix gently.

5. Spoon the filling into the avocado shells, sprinkle with the breadcrumbs and drizzle the butter over the top.

6. Dust with the paprika and bake at 400°F for 15 minutes.

TIME: Preparation takes about 10 minutes, cooking takes 15 minutes.

COOK'S TIP: Do not prepare this dish too far in advance as the avocado may discolor.

SERVING IDEA: Serve with a little salad as an appetizer or a rice pilaff,
vegetables and tossed salad for a main course.

259

INDONESIAN-STYLE STUFFED PEPPERS

*For this adaptable recipe you can substitute
pine nuts or peanuts if you don't have cashews.*

SERVES 8 AS AN APPETIZER

2 tbsps olive oil
1 medium onion, peeled and chopped
1 clove garlic, crushed
2 tsps turmeric
1 tsp crushed coriander seed
4 tbsps flaked coconut
1½ cups mushrooms, chopped
¾ cup bulgar wheat
½ cup raisins
1¼ cups stock or water
2-3 tomatoes, skinned and chopped
½ cup cashew nuts
4 small green peppers, de-seeded and cut
    in half lenthways
2 tsps lemon juice
Stock for cooking

1. Heat the oil and fry the onion and garlic until lightly browned.

2. Add the turmeric, coriander and coconut, and cook gently for about 2 minutes.

3. Add the mushrooms and bulgar wheat and cook for a further 2 minutes.

4. Add the rest of the ingredients except the nuts, lemon juice, peppers, and cooking stock, and simmer gently for 15-20 minutes until the bulgar wheat is cooked.

5. Toast the cashew nuts in a dry frying pan until golden brown.

6. Blanch the peppers in boiling water for 3 minutes.

7. Mix the nuts and lemon juice with the rest of the ingredients and fill the peppers with the mixture.

8. Place the filled peppers on the bottom of a large casserole dish and pour stock around the peppers.

9. Cook at 350°F for 20 minutes.

10. Drain peppers and place on a hot plate to serve.

TIME: Preparation takes 20 minutes, cooking takes 45 minutes.

FREEZING: The cooked peppers will freeze well for up to 3 months.

ZUCCHINI AND PINE NUT LASAGNE WITH EGGPLANT SAUCE

*This unusual lasagne will leave your guests guessing
about the delicious combination of ingredients.*

SERVES 4

12 strips of whole-wheat lasagne
¾ cup pine nuts
2 tbsps butter
4 zucchini, trimmed and sliced
1½ cups ricotta cheese
½ tsp grated nutmeg
1 tbsp olive oil
1 large eggplant, sliced
⅔ cup water
2 tsps shoyu sauce (Japanese soy sauce)
¾ cup cheddar cheese, grated

1. Place the lasagne in a large roasting pan and completely cover with boiling water. Leave for 10 minutes and then drain.

2. Place the pine nuts in a dry pan and roast gently for 2 minutes. Set aside.

3. Melt the butter and cook the zucchini with a little water until just tender.

4. Combine the zucchini, pine nuts and ricotta cheese.

5. Add the nutmeg and mix together thoroughly.

6. In a separate pan, heat the olive oil and sauté the eggplant for 4 minutes.

7. Add the water and shoyu and simmer, covered, until soft.

8. Purée in a food processor, adding extra water if necessary.

9. Place 4 strips of lasagne on the bottom of a greased 3 pint rectangular dish and top with half the zucchini mixture.

10. Place 4 more strips of lasagne over the zucchini and add half the eggplant sauce followed by the rest of the zucchini.

11. Cover with the remaining lasagne and the rest of the sauce.

12. Sprinkle the grated cheese over the top and bake for 40 minutes at 375°F, until the cheese is golden brown.

TIME: Preparation takes about 30 minutes, cooking takes 50 minutes.

SERVING IDEA: Delicious served with a crunchy mixed salad and garlic bread or with one of the dishes in the Salads for all Seasons chapter.

PARSNIP ROAST

*This colorful roast is perfect for picnics
as well as entertaining.*

SERVES 4

1lb parsnips
1 tbsp freshly chopped tarragon
1 small onion, very finely chopped
2 eggs, beaten
Salt
Black pepper

1. Grease and line a 7½ x 4 inch loaf pan with wax paper.

2. Peel and slice the parsnips, cover with water and cook until soft.

3. Drain the parsnips, dry off over a low heat and mash well with a potato masher or fork.

4. Add the tarragon, onion, eggs and seasoning and mix together well.

5. Put the mixture into the loaf pan and smooth over the top with a knife.

6. Cover with foil and bake at 325°F for 1 hour.

TIME: Preparation takes 10 minutes, cooking takes about 1 hour.

SERVING IDEA: Garnish with fresh tarragon and slices of green pepper. Serve hot with a platter of mixed cooked vegetables – carrot sticks, cauliflower florets and sliced red and green peppers – or cold on a bed of lollo rosso or oak leaf lettuce with a carrot coleslaw.

VARIATION: Use 2 tbsps of chopped parsley if tarragon is not available.

COOK'S TIP: This loaf can be assembled earlier in the day and refrigerated until just before cooking.

ASPARAGUS AND OLIVE QUICHE

*An interesting combination which gives
a new twist to a classic dish.*

MAKES 2 QUICHES

2 x 10 inch part baked pastry shells
6 eggs
2½ cups cream
1 tsp salt
Pinch of nutmeg
Salt and pepper
2 tbsps flour
2 cans green asparagus tips
¾ cup green olives
2 onions, finely chopped and sautéed in a
    little butter until soft
¾ cup cheddar cheese, grated
2 tbsps Parmesan cheese
4 tbsps butter

1. Whisk the eggs with the cream.

2. Add the salt, nutmeg and seasoning.

3. Mix a little of the mixture with the flour until smooth, then add to the cream mixture.

4. Arrange the asparagus tips, olives and onion in the pastry shells and pour the cream mixture over the top.

5. Sprinkle with the grated cheddar and Parmesan.

6. Dot with the butter and bake at 375°F for 25 minutes.

7. Turn down the oven to 350°F for a further 15 minutes until the quiches are golden.

TIME: Preparation takes 20 minutes, cooking takes 40 minutes.

FREEZING: The quiches may be frozen but a slightly better result is obtained if you freeze the pastry shells and add the filling just before baking.

SRI LANKAN RICE

*Serve this rice hot as an accompaniment
to vegetable curries or pulse dishes.*

SERVES 12

3 tbsps sunflower oil
1 medium onion, finely chopped
2 cloves garlic, crushed
1 heaped tsp ground cumin
1 heaped tsp ground coriander
1 heaped tsp paprika
2 tsps turmeric
¼ tsp chili or cayenne pepper
⅔ cup Basmati rice, washed and drained
1½ cups skimmed milk
1 tsp salt
Ground pepper to taste
1 cup pea pods trimmed and cut in half
1½ cups mushrooms, washed and sliced
⅔ cup corn
½ cup raisins, washed and soaked

1. Heat the oil in a large non-stick pan.

2. Gently fry the onion and garlic for 4-5 minutes.

3. Add the cumin, coriander, paprika, turmeric and chili, and fry for a further 3-4 minutes – do not allow the mixture to burn.

4. Add the washed rice and mix well with the onions and spices for about 2 minutes.

5. Add the milk, salt and pepper, stir gently, bring to the boil, cover and simmer until all the liquid is absorbed and the rice is cooked – approximately 15-20 minutes.

6. While the rice is cooking, steam the pea pods, mushrooms, sweet and raisins and fold into the rice.

8. Serve immediately or transfer to a serving dish to cool.

TIME: Preparation takes 15 minutes, cooking takes 25-30 minutes.

SERVING IDEA: Sprinkle with 2 tbsps of freshly chopped coriander, parsley or chives.

VARIATION: Other lightly steamed vegetables may be used according to season and personal taste – broccoli florets, diced carrots, peas and sliced green peppers.

FESTIVE ROAST

*Never again will Christmas or Thanksgiving dinner
be a problem with this festive roast.*

SERVES 8

2 tbsps sunflower oil
2 medium onions, finely chopped
2 cloves garlic, crushed
4 cups finely ground cashew nuts
2 cups whole-wheat breadcrumbs
2 beaten eggs or 4 tbsps soya flour mixed
  with a little water
1 heaped tsp mixed herbs
2 tsps vegetable bouillon powder
1¼ cups boiling water
Salt and pepper

1. Heat the oil and fry the onion and garlic until soft.

2. Place the onions and garlic into a large bowl. Add all the other ingredients and mix well.

3. Grease and line a 9 x 5 inch loaf pan with wax paper and spoon in the mixture.

4. Cover with a double thickness of foil and cook in a preheated oven at 350°F for about 1 hour 20 minutes until firm.

5. Allow to cool for about 10 minutes in the pan before turning out.

TIME: Preparation takes about 15 minutes, cooking takes about 1 hour 20 minutes.

FREEZING: An excellent dish to freeze cooked or uncooked, although a slightly better result is obtained if frozen uncooked and thawed overnight in the refrigerator.

SERVING IDEA: Serve with a wine sauce or gravy, cranberry sauce and candied sweet potatoes or mashed potatoes.

CARROT AND PARSNIP MEDLEY

The perfect accompaniment to Festive Roast.

SERVES 8

⅓ cup butter
8 medium carrots, peeled and sliced
4 parsnips, peeled and cut into rounds
1 level tsp ground ginger
½ tsp grated nutmeg
Salt and pepper
Juice of 1 lemon
2 tsps fine sugar
Chopped parsley

1. Melt the butter in a large pan and add the carrots and parsnips.

2. Sauté very gently for 2-3 minutes then add the ginger, nutmeg, seasoning, lemon juice and enough water to cover the vegetables.

3. Cover and simmer for 15-20 minutes until the vegetables are soft and the liquid has evaporated.

4. Add the sugar and increase the heat, tossing the vegetables until they are glossy.

5. Transfer to a heated serving dish and sprinkle with the chopped parsley.

TIME: Preparation takes 10 minutes, cooking takes 20-25 minutes.

VARIATION: Any chopped fresh herbs may be used for garnishing – coriander is a good alternative.

COOK'S TIP: Lemons yield more juice if you first roll them backwards and forwards on a kitchen work surface with your hands using medium pressure.

MINCEMEAT TARTS

Bottled mincemeat is often available in specialist stores,
but check the label as some contain beef suet.

MAKES ABOUT 16

2 cups whole-wheat flour
2 tsps baking powder
Pinch of salt
½ cup margarine or butter
⅓ cup granulated brown sugar
Yolk of 1 egg
2 tbsps cold water
1-2 cups vegetarian mincemeat
A little milk

1. Combine flour and salt. Rub in margarine or butter until mixture resembles fine breadcrumbs. Mix in the sugar.

2. Beat egg yolk and water together and add to the flour mixture, mixing to form a firm dough.

3. Wrap and refrigerate for half an hour.

4. Roll out the pastry about ¼ inch thick and cut out fifteen 3 inch rounds for the bases and fifteen 2 inch rounds for the lids.

5. Grease 2½ inch muffin pans and line with the larger rounds. Half fill with mincemeat and cover with the lids, pressing lightly round the edges. Brush with milk and make steam holes in the tops.

6. Bake in a preheated oven 400°F for 20 minutes or until the pies are golden brown.

TIME: Preparation takes about 35 minutes, cooking takes 20-25 minutes.

FREEZING: The mince pies can be made well in advance and frozen for up to 3 months.

PREPARATION: To make a quick mincemeat filling combine ¾ cup raisins, 2 tbsps sherry or brandy 1½ cups finely chopped apples, 2 tbsps lemon juice, 2 tbsps orange juice, ½ cup candied orange peel, ½ cup brown sugar and ¼ tsp each ground cloves, mace and ginger. Refrigerate overnight before using.

TOFU SPINACH QUICHE

Serve this tasty flan with a medley of
lightly cooked fresh vegetables.

SERVES 4

Pie Crust
1 tsp brown sugar
2-3 tbsps water
2 tsps oil
1 cup whole-wheat flour
½ tsp baking powder
Pinch of salt
4 tbsps margarine

Filling
1½ cups spinach
2 cups tofu
Juice of 1 lemon
2 tbsps shoyu sauce (Japanese soy sauce)
4 tbsps sunflower oil
⅔ cup soy milk
Salt according to taste
¾ cup onions, chopped

1. Dissolve the sugar in the water and mix in the oil. Keep cool.

2. Mix the flour, baking powder and salt together in a large bowl.

3. Rub in the margarine until the mixture resembles fine breadcrumbs.

4. Add the liquid and mix into the flour, using more water if necessary. The dough should be of a wettish consistency.

5. Leave to rest under an inverted bowl for half an hour.

6. Preheat the oven to 375°F.

7. Roll out the dough to line a 7-8 inch pie dish.

8. Prick the base all over with a fork and bake blind for 5-6 minutes.

9. Wash the spinach, drain and cook in its own liquid in a covered pan until soft – about 5-8 minutes.

10. Drain the spinach, chop and set aside.

11. Crumble the tofu into a food processor, add the lemon juice, shoyu, 2 tbsps of the oil, the soy milk and salt. Blend to a thick creamy consistency. Adjust the seasoning if necessary.

12. Fry the chopped onions in the remaining oil until lightly browned.

13. Add the spinach and fold in the tofu cream.

14. Pour the mixture into the prepared pie shell and bake in the middle of the oven for 30 minutes or until set.

15. Allow to cool for about 10 minutes before serving.

TIME: Preparation takes 25 minutes, cooking takes 45 minutes.

WATCHPOINT: The filling may develop cracks on cooling but this is normal.

ENGLISH PLUM PUDDING

A traditional end to Christmas dinner in England.

SERVES 8

1 cup whole-wheat flour
1½ tsps baking powder
1 cup vegetarian suet
Grated rind of one small lemon
½ tsp grated nutmeg
1 cup golden raisins
2 cups raisins
1 cup candied cirtus peel
¼ cup chopped almonds
2 eggs, beaten
2 tbsps clear honey
⅔ cup milk

1. Combine the flour, baking powder and suet, add the lemon rind, nutmeg, fruit, peel and almonds.

2. Beat the eggs and whisk together with the honey.

3. Add to the dry ingredients with the milk and mix well.

4. Put into a greased heatproof bowl and cover with wax paper. Cover again with foil and tie tightly with string.

5. Place bowl in a saucepan with about 1 inch of boiling water and steam for 3 hours, adding more water as required.

6. Cool and wrap well in a clean kitchen towel. Store for between 4-6 weeks in the refrigerator.

7. On the day of serving, steam for a further 1½ hours before serving.

TIME: Preparation takes 40 minutes. Cooking takes 3 hours plus 1½ hours on the day of serving.

SERVING IDEA: Serve with hard sauce, a sweetened white sauce or coconut cream sauce.

VARIATION: If you can't find suet, use ⅔ cup cold butter cut into tiny dice.

CELEBRATION PUDDING

*This makes a delicious ending to Christmas dinner
and can be made for any celebration dinner.*

SERVES 8

First layer
½ cup golden raisins
½ cup raisins
1 cup dates
2 tbsps concentrated apple juice
1¼ cups fresh orange juice
Juice of ½ lemon
¼ tsp grated nutmeg
2 tbsps rum or brandy
½ cup chopped almonds

Second layer
2 cups dried apricots
1¼ cups fresh orange juice
Juice of ½ lemon
1 inch stick of cinnamon
½ cup ground almonds

Third layer
1¼ cups whipped cream
1 tbsp brandy (optional)

1. For the first layer, soak the golden raisins, raisins and dates in orange and lemon juice for 2 hours.

2. For the second layer, soak the apricots in the orange and lemon juice for 2 hours.

3. Simmer the apricots and fruit juice with the cinnamon stick for about 40 minutes or until the apricots are soft.

4. Remove the cinnamon stick, beat the apricots to a purée and stir in the ground almonds.

5. Simmer the golden raisins, raisins and dates in the apple juice, orange juice, lemon juice and nutmeg for about 40 minutes or until thick and syrupy.

6. Stir in the rum or brandy and the chopped almonds.

7. Stir the brandy into the whipped cream for the third layer.

8. Line a round bowl with plastic wrap and build the pudding up in layers beginning with the raisin mixture followed by the apricot mixture and lastly the whipped cream, making sure you end with a layer of the dark mixture on the top.

9. Cover and chill well.

10. Turn out onto a serving dish, remove the plastic wrap and flambé before serving.

TIME: Preparation takes 10 minutes, soaking takes 2 hours and cooking takes 40 minutes.

FREEZING: Freeze in the pudding basin for up to a month. Thaw at room temperature for 6 hours.

CHRISTMAS FRUIT CAKE

*This rich, moist fruit cake is made without sugar
or eggs and is suitable for vegans.*

½ cup clear honey
¾ cup safflower or sunflower oil
¾ cup soy flour
1¼ cups water
1 tbsp rum or 1 tsp rum extract
Grated rind and juice of 1 orange
Grated rind and juice of 1 lemon
½ cup flaked almonds
¾ cup dried figs, chopped
¾ cup dried dates, chopped
½ cup dried apricots, chopped
2 cups whole-wheat flour
3 tsps baking powder
Pinch salt
2 level tsps mixed spice
2 cups currants
2 cups golden raisins
2 cups raisins

1. Preheat the oven to 325°F. Line a 9 inch square cake pan with wax paper.

2. Beat the honey and the oil together.

3. Mix the soy flour with the water and gradually add to the oil and honey mixture, beating well.

4. Beat in the rum and the grated rind and juice of the orange and lemon. Add the almonds, figs, dates and apricots.

5. Mix the flour with the salt and spice and mix together the currants, golden raisins and raisins.

6. Stir half the flour and half the currant mixture into the soy cream, then stir in the remainder. Spoon into the prepared tin.

7. Cover with two or three layers of wax paper and bake for 3¼ to 3½ hours, or until a skewer inserted into the center comes out clean.

8. Cool for 10 minutes and turn out onto a wire rack to cool.

9. Keep in an airtight tin.

TIME: Preparation takes about 40 minutes, cooking takes 3¼ to 3½ hours.

COOK'S TIP: This cake will keep well but is best made three to four weeks before cutting and stored, wrapped in foil or wax paper, in an airtight tin.

SERVING IDEA: Leave plain or decorate with candied fruits.

VARIATION: Other dried fruits may be used instead of figs, dates and apricots but make sure that the overall measurements stay the same.

STRAWBERRY AND BANANA FROST

*This speedy dessert can be started ahead of
time and completed just before serving.*

SERVES 4-6

4 cups strawberries
1 large banana
¾ cup low fat cream cheese
¼ tsp vanilla extract
1 tsp clear honey

1. Wash and hull the strawberries and put half of them in the refrigerator.

2. Peel the banana and cut into pieces.

3. Cut the remaining strawberries in halves, quarters if they are large, and freeze with the banana until solid.

4. Just before serving, remove the strawberries and banana from the freezer.

5. Place the frozen strawberries, banana, cream cheese, vanilla extract and honey in a food processor or liquidiser and process until smooth. You will need to push the mixture down two or three times with a spatula or wooden spoon.

6. Divide the mixture between 4 or 6 individual serving dishes and place the remaining strawberries around the frost mixture.

7. Serve at once.

TIME: Preparation takes 10 minutes, freezing takes at least 1 hour.

VARIATION: Pineapple, raspberries or apple can be substituted.

285

HAWAIIAN PINEAPPLE PANCAKES

*You can try many different fruits as a
filling for these delicious pancakes.*

MAKES 12 PANCAKES

1½ cups flour
Pinch salt
2 small eggs, beaten
Scant 2 cups milk
1 tsp vegetable oil
2 tbsps cold water
Oil for frying

Filling
15oz can pineapple
1 cup cottage cheese
2-4 tsps sugar

1. Sift the flour and salt into a bowl.

2. Make a well in the center and add the beaten eggs.

3. Gradually beat in half the milk and mix until smooth.

4. Stir in oil, cold water and enough milk to make a thin batter.

5. Refrigerate for at least 1 hour.

6. Place a little oil into a 6 inch frying pan and heat until just smoking, pour in 2 tbsps of the batter and swirl round until the bottom is evenly coated.

7. Cook until the underside is golden, flip over and repeat.

8. Cool on a wire rack.

9. Repeat this process until all the batter has been used.

10. The pancakes can be frozen at this stage and filled just before cooking by interleaving them with wax paper and wrapping well with foil.

11. To make the filling, drain the pineapple and chop finely. Sieve the cottage cheese.

12. Mix the pineapple, cheese and sugar together. Divide equally between the pancakes and roll up around the filling.

13. Place in a single layer in an ovenproof dish. Cover with foil and freeze.

14. To serve, remove the wrapping and thaw at room temperature for 2-3 hours.

15. Reheat at 400°F for 20 minutes until heated through.

TIME: Preparation takes 10 minutes, cooking takes about 40 minutes.

SERVING IDEA: Serve the pancakes garnished with hot pineapple rings.

BRANDIED ORANGES WITH PEACH AND MANGO CREAM

An attractive dessert which tastes as good as it looks.

SERVES 4

6 large oranges
3 tbsps brandy
2 mangoes, peeled and cut into chunks
4 small ripe peaches, peeled and roughly
   chopped
3 tbsps heavy cream

1. Finely pare the peel from 3 of the oranges and boil it in a little water for 2 minutes.

2. Remove and cool.

3. Peel the oranges using a sharp knife, making sure that all the pith is removed.

4. Slice thinly, arrange the slices in a serving dish and sprinkle the peel over the top.

5. Sprinkle the brandy over the top and refrigerate for about an hour.

6. Put the mangoes and peaches into a food processor and blend until smooth.

7. Stir in the cream and refrigerate until required.

8. Pass the peach and mango cream when serving the oranges.

TIME: Preparation takes 20 minutes, cooking takes 2 minutes.

VARIATION: Yogurt may be used instead of heavy cream or it may be omitted altogether.

COOK'S TIP: Use a zester to remove the peel from the oranges.

CAROB SUNDAE

A delightful treat which provides the perfect end to any meal.

SERVES 4

Carob Dessert
1 cup milk or soy milk
1 tsp pure vanilla extract
1 tbsp sunflower oil
2 tbsps honey
¼ tsp sea salt
1 tbsp cornstarch
¼ tsp instant coffee
1 tbsp carob powder

Vanilla Custard
1 tbsp cornmeal
½ cup milk or soya milk
1 tbsp honey
½ tsp pure vanilla extract

Filling
1 large banana, chopped
2 cups strawberries, hulled, washed
   and halved.

1. Blend all the carob dessert ingredients together in a saucepan and cook until thick, stirring continuously.

2. Leave to cool.

3. Mix the cornmeal with a little of the milk to make a smooth paste and add the honey and vanilla essence.

4. Heat the remaining milk until nearly boiling and pour over the cornmeal mixture, stirring until smooth.

5. Return to the pan and re-heat gently until thick, stirring constantly.

6. Leave to cool.

7. Add half the carob dessert to the chopped banana and mix together carefully.

8. Fill sundae glasses with layers of carob dessert, banana mixture, strawberries, vanilla custard and finally the plain carob dessert.

9. Chill before serving.

TIME: Preparation takes about 20 minutes, cooking takes 10 minutes.

SERVING IDEA: Serve decorated with grated coconut.

VARIATION: Raspberries can be used if strawberries are not available.

FRUIT FANTASIA

A pretty dessert which is simple to prepare and perfectly refreshing.

SERVES 8

1 melon
4 large grapefruit
1 cup black grapes
1 cup green grapes
2 red apples
1 small carton cream
Mint leaves for garnishing

1. Cut the melon into quarters. Remove the flesh, cut into 1-inch pieces and place in a large bowl.

2. Make zig-zag cuts around each grapefruit, halve, remove the flesh and add to the melon, reserving the grapefruit shells.

3. Remove the seeds from the grapes and cut into halves.

4. Wash the apples and slice finely, leaving the skin on. Add to the grapefruit, grapes and melon.

5. Chill for at least an hour.

6. Mix the cream carefully into the fruit and pile into the grapefruit shells.

7. Garnish with the mint before serving.

TIME: Preparation takes about 10 minutes, chilling takes at least one hour.

SERVING IDEA: Serve in individual dishes containing crushed ice and garnished with mint leaves.

VARIATION: If time is short use seedless grapes and leave whole.

DESSERTS

"The proof of the pudding is in the eating".
Henry Glapthorne
The Hollander 1635

By far and away the healthiest and easiest dessert to serve is fresh fruit. A bowl filled with a wide selection of fruits in season provides a wonderful centerpiece for any dessert table. There are many occasions, however, when delicious home-made desserts cannot be beaten. Ice cream is one of the most popular and is well worth making in large quantities when fresh fruit is cheap and plentiful. There is also that wonderful alternative to rich ice-creams – yogurt.

If you are making a pie or pastry dish, it is just as easy to make two, three of even four and freeze them for a later date. Should unexpected guests turn up, everyday pudding can be transformed by the addition of a few chopped nuts and whipped cream piped around the dish. Serve light desserts at the end of a filling main meal and more substantial puddings, such as cheesecake, after a light meal or salad. And if you are short of time don't forget that a mixed cheese platter is a delicious finale and you'll find a wide range of vegetarian cheeses are available at many supermarkets as well as specialist cheese shops.

FLAMBÉED CARAMEL CUSTARDS

The perfect dinner party dessert.

SERVES 6

Caramel
½ cup soft brown sugar
4 tbsps water

Custards
3 eggs
½ cup finely ground soft brown sugar
Scant 2 cups milk
A pinch mixed spice
Thinly pared rind of 1 orange
⅔ cup brandy

1. Melt the sugar in the water over a moderate heat and boil until it begins to turn golden brown.

2. Remove from the heat and divide the mixture to coat the base of six custard cups.

3. Whisk the eggs and add the sugar.

4. Put the milk into a saucepan with the spice and orange rind and heat until simmering.

5. Add to the eggs and mix well.

6. Pour equal quantities of custard in the custard cups and place them in a deep roasting pan.

7. Pour in enough water to come up to about two thirds of the sides of the custard cups.

8. Bake at 300°F for about 1 hour or until the custard has set.

9. Turn out onto a hot serving dish.

10. Heat the brandy in a ladle or small pan and ignite for about 10 seconds.

11. Pour over the custards and serve immediately.

TIME: Preparation takes 5 minutes, cooking takes about 1 hour.

297

WINDWARD FRUIT BASKET

An impressive dessert which is surprisingly easy to prepare.

SERVES 4-6

1 large ripe melon
2 apples
Juice of 1 lime
2 mangoes
2 kiwi fruit
2 cups strawberries
1 cup raspberries
3 tbsps honey
2 tbsps dark rum
4 tbsps butter

1. Cut the top off the melon and scoop out the seeds.

2. Using a melon baller, scoop out balls of melon and place in a large bowl.

3. Remove the core from the apples, dice and toss in the lime juice.

4. Peel and chop the mangoes.

5. Peel and slice the kiwi fruit.

6. Combine all the fruits.

7. Heat the honey, rum and butter gently until the butter has melted.

8. Cool, and pour over the fruits.

9. Toss gently and fill the melon shell with the fruit mixture.

10. Place on a serving dish and serve immediately.

TIME: Preparation takes 20 minutes, cooking takes 2 minutes.

SERVING IDEA: For a special occasion, make holes around the top of the melon with a skewer and decorate with fresh flowers.

VARIATION: Use any fresh fruits in season, pears, peaches etc.

STRAWBERRY SHERBET

*Serve at the end of a very rich meal or between the main
course and dessert during a light summer dinner.*

SERVES 4

1 medium lemon
1¼ cups water
¾ cup sugar
3 cups strawberries
2 egg whites

1. Pare the lemon rind from the lemon and put into the water with the sugar.

2. Heat slowly until the sugar has dissolved then boil for 5 minutes.

3. Strain and set aside to cool.

4. Hull the strawberries reserving a few for decoration. Press the remainder through a strainer and add the juice of half the lemon.

5. Whisk the egg whites until very stiff.

6. Combine all the ingredients well.

7. Put into a container and place in the freezer.

8. Remove when half frozen, beat well and return to the freezer.

9. Place in the refrigerator about 1 hour before serving.

10. Serve in wine glasses topped with the whole berries.

TIME: Preparation takes 20 minutes, cooking takes 5 minutes.
Freezing takes about 8 hours.

COOK'S TIP: It is better to leave the sherbet in the freezer overnight at the end of Step 8.

BROWN BREAD FROZEN YOGURT

This frozen dessert is ideal for dieters.

SERVES 4

⅓ cup brown breadcrumbs
⅓ cup brown sugar
3 eggs, separated
1¼ cups thick set plain yogurt
2 tsps honey (optional)

1. Place the breadcrumbs on a cookie sheet and cover with the sugar.

2. Place in a moderately hot oven 375°F for 20 minutes or until they begin to brown and caramelize. Stir once or twice so they brown evenly. Set aside to cool.

3. Beat the egg whites until stiff.

4. In a separate bowl, mix the egg yolks into the yogurt and then fold in the egg whites. Add the honey if desired and fold in evenly.

5. Add the cold breadcrumbs and mix well.

6. Place in the freezer and when ice crystals form beat well until smooth.

7. Return to the freezer and leave until set.

TIME: Preparation takes 20 minutes, cooking and freezing takes 20 minutes plus 4-5 hours or overnight.

COOK'S TIP: Remove from the freezer and place in the refrigerator about ¾ of an hour before serving.

VARIATION: Maple syrup may be used in place of honey.

BROWN BREAD FROZEN YOGURT

This frozen dessert is ideal for dieters.

SERVES 4

⅓ cup brown breadcrumbs
⅓ cup brown sugar
3 eggs, separated
1¼ cups thick set plain yogurt
2 tsps honey (optional)

1. Place the breadcrumbs on a cookie sheet and cover with the sugar.

2. Place in a moderately hot oven 375°F for 20 minutes or until they begin to brown and caramelize. Stir once or twice so they brown evenly. Set aside to cool.

3. Beat the egg whites until stiff.

4. In a separate bowl, mix the egg yolks into the yogurt and then fold in the egg whites. Add the honey if desired and fold in evenly.

5. Add the cold breadcrumbs and mix well.

6. Place in the freezer and when ice crystals form beat well until smooth.

7. Return to the freezer and leave until set.

TIME: Preparation takes 20 minutes, cooking and freezing takes 20 minutes plus 4-5 hours or overnight.

COOK'S TIP: Remove from the freezer and place in the refrigerator about ¾ of an hour before serving.

VARIATION: Maple syrup may be used in place of honey.

COFFEE AND RAISIN ICE CREAM

Perfect for a sweet finale or just as a treat.

MAKES 1 pint

1¼ cup milk
½ cup sugar
6 tsps instant coffee
1 tsp cocoa
1 egg yolk
1 tsp vanilla extract
1¼ cups whipping cream
¼ cup raisins

1. Heat the milk and sugar until almost boiling.

2. Add the coffee and cocoa, stir and leave to cool.

3. Beat the egg yolk with the vanilla extract until frothy.

4. Whip the cream until stiff.

5. Pour the cream and coffee mixture into the egg mixture and stir well.

6. Add the raisins and stir again.

7. Freeze until firm (3-4 hours), stirring several times during freezing.

8. Defrost for 10-15 minutes before serving.

TIME: Preparation takes 3-4 hours, including freezing.

SERVING IDEA: Serve with home-made cookies.

VARIATION: For a chocolate flavor use light carob powder in place of coffee.

CASHEW ICE CREAM

*For special occasions, just add 1 tbsp of rum for
an even more impressive ice-cream.*

SERVES 4

1 large very ripe banana, peeled and
   roughly chopped
1 cup finely ground cashew nuts
⅔ cup concentrated soy milk
½ tsp vanilla extract
2 tsps clear honey
2 rings unsweetened canned pineapple,
   diced

1. Put all the ingredients, apart from the pineapple, into a blender and blend until smooth.

2. Add the pineapple and blend briefly.

3. Put the mixture in a shallow container and freeze for 2 hours.

TIME: Preparation takes 10 minutes, freezing takes 2 hours.

SERVING IDEA: Serve with strawberries or fresh fruit salad.

APRICOT SNOW

Serve this light dessert in individual serving glasses,
and decorate with curls of carob.

SERVES 2-4

2 cups dried apricots
1 ripe banana
1 small carton plain yogurt, strained
  overnight
1 egg
Few squares carob

1. Soak the apricots in water for at least 1 hour. Cook until soft then purée.

2. Mash the banana and add to the apricot purée.

3. Fold the yogurt into the fruit mixture.

4. Separate the egg and stir the yolk into fruit mixture.

5. Whisk the egg white until stiff then fold into the fruit mixture.

TIME: Preparation takes 10 minutes. Soaking and cooking takes about 2 hours 40 minutes.

VARIATION: Decorate with toasted almonds.

COOK'S TIP: Line a strainer with cheesecloth and place over a bowl.
Empty the yogurt into the strainer and refrigerate overnight.
The liquid will drain away leaving the yogurt very thick.

CRANBERRY CREAM

A simple and refreshing dessert.

SERVES 4

2 cups fresh cranberries
2-4 tbsps clear honey
⅓ cup whipping cream
½ cup thick set plain yogurt
Toasted sliced almonds

1. Rinse the cranberries and stew with a scant amount of water until softened.

2. Remove from the heat, add the honey to taste and leave to cool.

3. Whip the cream and gently fold in the yogurt.

4. Combine the yogurt and cream with the cooled cranberries.

5. Divide the mixture between four stem glasses and decorate with toasted almonds.

TIME: Preparation takes 10 minutes, cooking takes 15-20 minutes.

VARIATION: As fresh cranberries are not available year round, redcurrants or raspberries can also be used.

LEMON TART

A classic dessert, loved by all age groups.

SERVES 6-8

½ cup vegetable fat
2 cups whole-wheat flour
¼ cup brown sugar
2 egg yolks
A little water

Filling
4 egg yolks
4 egg whites beaten
½ cup brown sugar
½ cup ground almonds
½ cup sweet butter, softened
⅔ cup cream, slightly whipped
2 lemons, rind and juice

1. Rub the fat into the flour until the mixture resembles fine breadcrumbs.

2. Mix in the sugar, add the egg yolks and a little water to mix.

3. Roll out to line a fairly deep flan tin.

4. Prick the bottom and bake blind in the oven for about 8 minutes at 425°F.

5. Meanwhile, mix the egg yolks with the sugar and add the ground almonds, butter, whipped cream and lemon juice.

6. Beat until smooth and creamy and fold in the lemon rind and beaten egg whites.

7. Pour into the pastry case and bake 350°F until slightly risen and golden brown.

8. Chill before serving.

TIME: Preparation takes 25 minutes, cooking takes 48 minutes.

SERVING IDEA: Serve decorated with piped whipped cream.

WATCHPOINT: Do not overbeat the filling as it is liable to overflow during cooking.

ORANGE AND KIWI CHEESECAKE

Lemon could be used in place of orange if a tangy cheesecake is required.

SERVES 6-8

½ cup margarine
2 cups crushed graham crackers

Topping
2 cups low fat cream cheese
½ cup margarine
1 medium egg, beaten
Fruit and zest of 1 orange, chopped
¼ cup ground almonds
¼ tsp almond extract
2 kiwi fruit

1. Make the base by melting the margarine and adding to the biscuit crumbs. Mix well and press into a dish or flan base.

2. Chill thoroughly.

3. Mix together the cheese, margarine, egg, chopped orange and zest, almonds, almond extract and one kiwi fruit, peeled and chopped.

4. Put onto crust and smooth over the top.

5. Peel and slice the other kiwi-fruit and decorate the top of the cheesecake.

6. Chill for 2 hours.

TIME: Preparation takes 15 minutes. Chilling takes 2 hours.

SERVING IDEA: For a special occasion decorate with the kiwi fruit and halved and seeded red grapes.

PEACHY CHEESECAKE

A quite rich cheesecake with a velvety texture.

SERVES 6

Crust
8 graham crackers, crushed or
   processed until fine
3 tbsps melted butter or margarine

Topping
1¼ cups cream cheese
Scant 2 cups sour cream
2 tbsps clear honey
1½ tsps vanilla extract or lemon juice
2 eggs, beaten
1½ tbsps self-rising flour
Sliced peaches to decorate

1. Preheat the oven to 300°F.

2. Combine the crumbs, melted butter and spices and press the mixture in the bottom of a greased 9 inch flan dish.

3. Combine the cream cheese and half of the sour cream, 1 tbsp honey, ¾ tsp vanilla extract, the eggs and all the flour.

4. Pour the mixture onto the crust and bake in the preheated oven for approximately 20 minutes or until just set.

5. Remove from the oven and increase the oven temperature to 450°F.

6. Combine the remaining sour cream with the rest of the honey and vanilla extract and spread over the top of the cake. Smooth over with a knife or spatula.

7. Return to the oven and bake for 5 minutes.

8. Allow to cool before decorating with sliced peaches.

9. Chill thoroughly before serving.

TIME: Preparation takes 25 minutes, cooking takes 25 minutes.

VARIATION: For special occasions decorate with seasonal fruit such as strawberries or raspberries and carob curls.

COOK'S TIP: Sugar-free canned fruit may be used if fresh is not available.

CORN CAKE

This corn cake will freeze well.

MAKES 1 CAKE

Scant 3 cups milk
4 tbsps brown sugar
½ tsp vanilla extract
1 cup fine cornmeal
2 eggs
Pinch of salt
4 tbsps margarine

1. Grease and line the bottom of a 7 inch spring-form pan with a circle of waxed paper.

2. Put the milk, sugar and vanilla extract into a saucepan and bring to the boil.

3. Stir in the cornmeal quickly to avoid forming lumps.

4. Remove the pan from the heat and allow to cool slightly.

5. Separate the eggs.

6. Beat the egg whites with a pinch of salt until it forms soft peaks.

7. Add the margarine and egg yolks, one at a time, to the cornmeal and beat well.

8. Stir in one spoonful of the egg white and then fold in the remainder carefully with a metal spoon.

9. Pour the mixture into a prepared tin and bake at 350°F for about 40 minutes.

10. Transfer the cake onto a wire rack to cool.

TIME: Preparation takes 15 minutes, cooking takes 40 minutes.

SERVING IDEA: Decorate the top with fresh fruit and sprinkle nuts on the sides.

CAROB APPLE CAKE

This cake is nicer if kept in an airtight container for a day before serving.

MAKES 1 CAKE

⅔ cup whipped margarine
½ cup light brown sugar
1 large egg, beaten
1½ cups fine whole-wheat flour
5 tbsps carob powder
1½ tsps baking powder
1 tbsp Amontillado sherry (medium dry)
2¾ cups apples, peeled and sliced

Topping
½ cup carob chips
1 tbsp butter
A little water

1. Cream the margarine and sugar together until fluffy.

2. Add half of the beaten egg and continue creaming.

3. Add the rest of the egg together with the flour, carob and baking powder and sherry.

4. Spoon half of the mixture into a round 8 inch cake pan and cover with the sliced apples.

5. Add the other half of the mixture and smooth the top.

6. Bake at 325°F for 1¼ hours or until firm to the touch.

7. Melt the carob chips with the butter and water and drizzle over the top of the cake.

TIME: Preparation takes 25 minutes, cooking takes 1¼ hours.

SERVING IDEA: Serve hot with yogurt or cold with tea or coffee.

DE-LUXE BREAD AND BUTTER PUDDING

Serve just as it is, hot from the oven.

SERVES 2-4

4 thin slices whole-wheat bread
A little butter
Raspberry jam
2 eggs, beaten
Scant 2 cups milk, warmed
2 tbsps cream
3 tbsps light brown sugar
1 tsp vanilla extract
2 tbsps raisins, soaked for 1 hour
1 tbsp dates
Grated nutmeg

1. Remove the crusts from the bread.

2. Sandwich the bread with the butter and jam and cut into small triangles.

3. Beat the eggs until fluffy.

4. Add the warmed milk, cream, sugar and vanilla.

5. Stir together well, making sure that the sugar has dissolved.

6. Arrange the bread triangles in a lightly buttered ovenproof dish so that they overlap and stand up slightly.

7. Scatter the dried fruits over the top.

8. Pour the egg, cream and milk mixture into the dish, ensuring that the bread triangles are saturated.

9. Grate a little nutmeg over the pudding and bake at 400°F for about 30 minutes.

TIME: Preparation takes 10 minutes, cooking takes 30 minutes.

VARIATION: Other flavored jams may be used instead of raspberry jam.

CRANBERRY AND APPLE CRISP

Serve hot with natural yogurt or serve cold with ice cream.

SERVES 4

1½ lbs cooking apples
¼ cup raw sugar
1½ cups fresh cranberries

Crumble
⅓ cup butter or margarine
½ cup sunflower seeds
⅓ cup raw cane or demerara sugar
1¼ cups whole-wheat flour
1 cup oatmeal

1. Peel, core and dice the apples. Measure about 4¾ cups.

2. Cook in a saucepan with the sugar and about 2 tbsps water until slightly softened.

3. Add the cranberries and cook for a further minute. Remove from the heat.

4. Melt butter or margarine and add the sunflower seeds. Fry gently for a few minutes.

5. Meanwhile, mix together the other ingredients in a large bowl, rubbing in the sugar if lumpy.

6. Pour in the butter and sunflower seeds and combine to form a loose mixture.

7. Place the fruit in a large, shallow oven-proof dish and sprinkle the crisp topping over.

8. Cook at 350°F for about 40 minutes or until the top is golden and crisp.

TIME: Preparation takes about 20 minutes, cooking takes 50 minutes.

RICE MERINGUE

*For convenience the rice pudding and apple purée can be
made in advance and assembled just before cooking the meringue.*

SERVES 4

¼ cup short grain pudding rice
2 cups milk
¼ tsp almond extract
5 tbsps soft brown sugar
A little butter
2 large apples
2 tbsps raspberry jam
2 egg whites

1. Wash the rice and put into a shallow, buttered ovenproof dish.

2. Add the milk, almond extract and 2 tbsps of soft brown sugar.

3. Dot with a little butter and bake for 2½ -3 hours at 325°F stirring two or three times during cooking.

4. Remove from the oven.

5. Meanwhile, peel and core the apples. Slice finely and put into a saucepan with 1 tbsp of water.

6. Cook for 5-10 minutes until softened.

7. Add a little of the sugar to sweeten.

8. Cover the rice pudding with the raspberry jam.

9. Spread the apple purée over the top.

10. Beat the egg whites until they are stiff but not dry.

11. Beat the remaining sugar gradually into the egg whites and cover the pudding with the meringue mixture.

12. With the back of a spoon, pull the meringue into peaks.

13. Bake at 325°F for 20-30 minutes until heated through and golden on top.

14. Serve immediately.

TIME: Preparation takes 20 minutes, overall cooking takes about 3½ hours.

VARIATION: Make in individual ovenproof dishes.

HOT APPLE PIZZA

A delicious dessert – perfect with yogurt or cream.

SERVES 4-6

1 tbsp fresh or active dry yeast
¼ cup warm water, hand hot
¾ cup strong whole-wheat bread flour
½ cup white bread flour
½ tsp ground cinnamon
1 tbsp butter or margarine
½ tbsp concentrated apple juice

Topping
2 red skinned apples
¼ cup raisins
¼ cup hazelnuts
1 tbsp concentrated apple juice
1 tbsp butter or margarine

1. Mix the yeast with the water, add 1 teaspoon of flour and leave in a warm place for 10-15 minutes until frothy.

2. Mix together the flours and cinnamon.

3. Rub in the butter.

4. Add the yeast mixture and concentrated apple juice to the flour.

5. Mix to a stiff dough, adding more warm water if necessary. Knead well.

6. Roll the dough into a circle, about 8 to 9 inches in diameter. Cover and leave to rise for 10-15 minutes.

7. Slice the apples evenly and arrange over the crust.

8. Sprinkle the raisins, hazelnuts and concentrated apple juice over the apples and dot with the butter or margarine.

9. Bake on the middle shelf of the oven at 400°F for 15-20 minutes.

TIME: Preparation takes, including rising, 45 minutes. Cooking takes 15-20 minutes.

VARIATION: Use other fruits, such as peaches, plums, pears or nectarines in place of the apples.

PEAR AND APRICOT SLICE

Serve as a dessert topped with thick set yogurt, or plain with coffee or tea.

MAKES 8 SLICES

2 pears
1 cup dried apricots, soaked
1 tbsp clear honey
½ tbsp pear and apple spread
1 tbsp sunflower oil
1 egg
1 cup whole-wheat flour
1 tsp baking powder
Sliced almonds to decorate

1. Peel and chop the pears into small pieces.

2. Chop the apricots finely.

3. Mix together the honey, pear and apple spread, and stir into the pears and apricots.

4. Add the oil and egg and mix well.

5. Mix together the flour and baking powder and fold into the pear and apricot mixture.

6. Spread the mixture in a greased 6 x 8 inch tin.

7. Sprinkle with the sliced almonds.

8. Bake at 375°F for about 25 minutes or until risen and golden.

9. Leave to cool and cut into 8 fingers.

TIME: Preparation takes about 15 minutes, cooking takes 25 minutes.

COOK'S TIP: Pear and Apple Spread is sugar free and can be bought at most health food stores. It is an ideal substitute for jam. Other flavors of fruit spread are also available.

BAKED RASPBERRY APPLES

A lovely combination which is perfectly complemented by cream or yogurt.

SERVES 6

---

2 tbsps concentrated apple juice
4 tbsps water
2 tbsps honey
1 tsp mixed spice
3 large apples
2 cups raspberries

---

1. Put the concentrated apple juice, water, honey and mixed spice into a large bowl and mix together well.

2. Wash the apples and, with a sharp knife, make deep zig-zag cuts around each apple.

3. Take one half of the apple in each hand and twist gently until the two halves come apart.

4. Remove the core and immerse each apple in the apple juice mixture.

5. Place the apples in an ovenproof dish and bake at 400°F for 20-25 minutes until just soft.

6. Remove from the oven and top with the raspberries.

7. Pour the remaining apple juice mixture over the raspberries and return to the oven, at 300°F for 10 minutes.

8. Serve at once.

TIME: Preparation takes 10 minutes, cooking takes 30-35 minutes.

SERVING IDEA: Serve topped with a spoonful of plain yogurt or whipped cream.

COOK'S TIP: Frozen raspberries may be used but make sure they are well thawed out.

CAROB PEARS

Children in particular will love these tasty pears.

SERVES 4

4 ripe pears
1 tbsp maple syrup
Boiling water to cover
1 cup carob bar, chopped
¼ cup grated coconut

1. Peel the pears thinly, leaving on the stalks.

2. Cut a small slice from the base of each pear so they will stand upright, and place in a bowl.

3. Mix the maple syrup with the boiling water and pour over the pears. Leave to go cold.

4. Remove the pears from the syrup and dry carefully. Place in one large or four small serving dishes.

5. Place the chopped carob bar in a small heatproof bowl.

6. Stand the bowl in a saucepan of boiling water until carob melts, stirring from time to time.

7. Spoon the melted carob over the pears, allow to set a little before sprinkling the coconut over the top.

8. Refrigerate for 2-3 hours.

TIME: Preparation takes 10 minutes, cooling takes 30 minutes.

SERVING IDEA: Serve with cream or yogurt.

FRUIT COCKTAIL TRIFLE

*Since you'll only need one of the sponge cakes for
the trifle, freeze the other to use later.*

SERVES 6

Carob Sponge Cake
½ cup whipped margarine
⅓ cup light brown sugar
2 eggs (size 3)
¾ cup whole-wheat flour, sifted
¼ cup carob powder
1½ tsps baking powder

Trifle
6 tbsps apple juice
Apricot or banana liqueur (optional)
2 apples, cored and chopped but not
    skinned
1 large banana, sliced
2 oranges, peeled, segmented and roughly
    chopped
Half a pineapple, diced
½ cup dates, chopped
½ cup hazelnuts
½ cup whipping cream
½ cup plain yogurt
Few grapes, halved and de-seeded

1. Cream the margarine and sugar together
until pale and fluffy.

2. Add the eggs, one at a time, then
carefully fold in the flour, carob powder
and baking powder.

3. Turn into two greased 7 inch cake pans
and bake for 20 minutes at 350°F until
golden brown and risen.

4. Leave to cool.

5. Place one of the carob cakes into a
glass bowl and saturate with the apple
juice. Leave for half an hour.

6. Add the liqueur, fruits and nuts, making
sure they are equally distributed through
the bowl.

7. Whip the cream until stiff and fold in
the yogurt.

8. Spread over the trifle.

9. With the back of a fork, trace from the
rim of the bowl into the center, making a
lined pattern.

10. Chill before serving.

TIME: Preparation takes 30 minutes, cooking takes 30 minutes.

SERVING IDEA: Serve decorated with orange segments, pineapple cubes and carob chips.

CARIBBEAN PINEAPPLE

An impressive and delicious dessert which is easy to prepare.

SERVES 6-8

1 large fresh pineapple
⅔ cup heavy cream
1 quantity of Coffee and Raisin Ice-Cream (see index)
½ cup rum
2 tbsps chopped mixed nuts

1. Slice the top off the pineapple at the shoulder and scoop out the flesh from the top.

2. Using a sharp knife, cut just within the skin around the circumference almost to the bottom.

3. Insert the blade 1 inch up from the base and cut round in both directions just enough to loosen the flesh. Do not cut the bottom off.

4. Insert a fork into the top of the pineapple flesh and twist to remove. Drain the cask and place in the freezer.

5. Remove the hard core from the pineapple and chop the flesh into tiny pieces, drain well.

6. Whip the cream until stiff.

7. In a large bowl, break up the ice-cream with a wooden spoon.

8. Add the cream, nuts and chopped pineapple and mix well.

9. Sprinkle this mixture with half of the rum.

10. Fill the frozen pineapple shell with the mixture, replace the top and wrap carefully in foil.

11. Return to the freezer until required. Any extra mixture can be frozen in a small bowl.

12. To serve, transfer the pineapple to the refrigerator three quarters of an hour before required.

13. Place a serving dish in the oven to become very hot.

14. Put the pineapple on hot dish, pour the rest of the rum onto the dish and a little on the sides of the shell and light it.

15. Scoop out a portion of the ice-cream into individual serving dishes and spoon over a little burnt rum.

TIME: Preparation takes 20 minutes.

VARIATION: Use plain vanilla ice-cream and add 1 tablespoonful of instant coffee and ¼ cup of raisins to the whipped cream.

BANANA FLAVORED APRICOTS WITH COCONUT CREAM

Make this dessert a day ahead and serve straight from the fridge.

SERVES 4

2 cups dried apricots
1¼ cups banana flavored soy milk
   plus 3 extra tbsps
⅔ cup water
1 cup coconut, grated
Juice of ½ lemon

1. Chop the apricots finely and put into a bowl.

2. Pour the soy milk over the top.

3. Heat the water in a pan and stir in the coconut until it has softened. Allow to cool a little.

4. Put the coconut, lemon juice and 3 tbsps soya milk into a blender and blend until smooth.

5. Cover the apricots and cream with plastic wrap and refrigerate overnight.

TIME: Preparation takes 10 minutes, cooking takes 2 minutes. Refrigerate overnight.

SERVING IDEA: Serve in individual serving dishes topped with spoonfuls of whipped cream.

VARIATION: Plain soy milk may be used if the banana flavor is not available.

MINTED GRAPES

A refreshing dessert to serve after a large meal.

SERVES 4

3 cups green grapes
A little Creme de Menthe
⅔ cup sour cream
Soft brown sugar

1. Halve and de-seed the grapes.

2. Divide the grapes equally between four serving glasses.

3. Sprinkle with a little Creme de Menthe.

4. Top with sour cream.

5. Sprinkle a little brown sugar over and serve at once.

TIME: Preparation takes 10 minutes.

SERVING IDEA: Serve garnished with mint leaves.

VARIATION: Use sherry in place of the Creme de Menthe and yogurt instead of sour cream.

GINGER LOG

Omit the sherry from this dish and it becomes the perfect kid's treat.

SERVE 6

7oz pack ginger snaps
4 tbsps sherry
1¼ cups heavy cream
8oz can pineapple pieces
Chopped nuts, toasted

1. Remove any broken ginger snaps.

2. Pour a little sherry or use the juice from the pineapple into a small bowl.

3. Whip the cream until thick and divide into two.

4. Drain the pineapple pieces, divide into two and chop one half very finely.

5. Mix into half of the cream.

6. Briefly, dip each biscuit into the sherry or juice and, using the cream and pineapple mixture, sandwich the ginger snaps together to make a log.

7. Lay the log on a serving dish and cover with the other half of the whipped cream spreading evenly with a knife.

8. Refrigerate for at least 2 hours.

9. Sprinkle with chopped nuts and decorate with the remaining pineapple chunks.

TIME: Preparation takes 10 minutes. Refrigeration takes 2 hours.

SERVING IDEA: Cut diagonally to serve.

VARIATION: Sprinkle with toasted coconut instead of nuts.

STRAWBERRY CLOUD

It takes no time at all to make this delightful summer dessert.

SERVES 4-6

3 cups strawberries
1½ cups silken tofu
Juice of ½ lemon
2 tbsps soft brown sugar
¼ tsp vanilla extract

1. Wash and hull the strawberries. Leave a few on one side to decorate.

2. Drain the tofu and put into a food processor together with the strawberries, lemon juice and sugar.

3. Process until smooth.

4. Add vanilla extract to taste and mix well.

5. Divide the mixture between 4-6 individual serving dishes and decorate with the reserved strawberries.

6. Chill until required.

TIME: Preparation takes 5-8 minutes.

SERVING IDEA: For a special occasion, pipe whipped cream around the edges of the serving dishes.

VARIATION: Other fruits such as plums, peaches or raspberries may be used instead.

CHERRY BERRY MEDLEY

A pretty combination, perfect for summer lunches.

SERVES 6-8

Scant 2 cups water
½ cup soft brown sugar
1 tsp mixed spice
2 cups redcurrants
4 cups strawberries
2 cups raspberries
2 cups cherries, pitted

1. Put the water, sugar and spice into a pan.

2. Boil for 5 minutes.

3. Put the redcurrants into a heatproof bowl and pour over the boiling liquid.

4. Leave to cool.

5. When cold, add the strawberries, raspberries and cherries.

6. Stir well and refrigerate for at least 2 hours before serving.

TIME: Preparation takes 10 minutes, cooking takes 5 minutes. Cooling and refrigeration takes 2 hours 15 minutes.

SERVING IDEA: Serve with ice-cream and wafer cookies.

VARIATION: If using blueberries in place of redcurrants, treat in the same way.

KOMPOT (DRIED FRUIT SALAD)

This classic Middle Eastern dish is simple
to prepare and can be made well in advance.

SERVES 6-8

2 cups dried prunes
2 cups dried apricots
1 cup dried figs
1 cup raisins
1 cup blanched almonds
½ cup pine kernels
1 tsp cinnamon
¼ tsp nutmeg
½ cup brown sugar
1 tbsp rose extract (optional)
Juice and zest of 1 orange

1. Stone the prunes if necessary and chop roughly.

2. Halve the apricots and quarter the figs.

3. Place them in a large bowl and add the rest of the ingredients.

4. Cover with cold water.

5. Stir well and keep in a cool place for 1-2 days, stirring a couple of times each day.

6. Before serving, mix again well.

TIME: Preparation takes 15 minutes. Standing time 1-2 days.

SERVING IDEA: Place the mixture in a glass serving dish, and serve with yogurt or cream.

COOK'S TIP: After 24 hours the liquid in which the Kompot is soaking will become very thick and syrupy. If you need to add more liquid, add a little orange juice.

VARIATION: Other dried fruits may be used in the same quantities. Pistachio nuts can take the place of blanched almonds.

BAKING

There is something very satisfying about producing batches of home-made bread, cookies and cakes, even if they get eaten before they have time to cool down!

Wholefood cooking means using wholegrain and wholewheat flours. 100 per cent wholewheat or wholegrain flours are suitable for making breads, dough and heavier cakes, whereas 80-90 per cent flours have a finer texture and are suitable for pastries, cakes, scones and cookies.

Most recipes using white flour can be easily adapted by replacing all or some of it with wholewheat flour. To begin with it may be best trying half white flour and half brown as this will give an idea of the different tastes and textures you can achieve by altering the flours. If you like the mixture of half brown half white, then stick with this, if not then adapt it to suit your taste.

Fats are important in baking and the only restriction for vegetarians are lard and blends of both vegetable and animal fats. This restriction is really a health advantage since most fats and oils of vegetable origin are unsaturated, while those from animals are more highly saturated.

MRS. MURPHY'S WHOLEWHEAT BROWN BREAD

This is a very moist bread which will last for days.

MAKES 2 LOAVES

6 cups whole-wheat flour
1 cup white flour
1 cup bran flakes
2 cups oatmeal
½ cup wheatgerm
½ tsp baking soda
½ tsp sea salt
5 cups milk
2 eggs, beaten

1. Heat the oven to 350°F.

2. Mix all the dry ingredients together.

3. Mix the eggs and milk and add to the dry ingredients.

4. Spoon into 2 greased 7½ x 4 inch loaf pans and bake in the center of the oven for 1¼ to 1½ hours.

5. Turn out to cool on a wire rack.

TIME: Preparation takes about 20 minutes, cooking takes 1¼ to 1½ hours.

VARIATION: A handful of caraway seeds can be added to the mixture and some sprinkled on the top before baking.

QUICK HOME-MADE BREAD

*The molasses in this recipe gives the
bread an attractive color.*

MAKES 3 LOAVES

5 cups hand hot water
1 tbsp molasses
1 tbsp sunflower oil
13½ cups whole-wheat flour
2 pkgs fast action yeast
3 tsps sea salt

1. Set the oven to 425°F.

2. Oil three 9 x 5 inch bread pans and set them in a warm place.

3. Pour the hand hot water into 2 glass measuring cups.

4. Add the molasses and oil to one of the cups, mix and set aside.

5. Place the flour, yeast and salt into a large bowl and mix together thoroughly.

6. Gradually pour the water and molasses mixture into the flour, mixing in with your hands.

7. Add the other cup of water bit by bit until the dough is wettish but not sticky. You may have some water left over.

8. Knead the dough about 10 minutes.

9. Divide the dough between the three pans and press down firmly.

10. Leave to rise in a warm place for about 1 hour or until the dough has risen to the top of the pans.

11. Bake in the preheated oven for 35-40 minutes.

TIME: Preparation takes 20 minutes plus rising, cooking takes 35-40 minutes.

FREEZING: This bread will freeze well.

RICH POPPY SEED ROLL

*A favorite sweet bread at Christmas time, this is
Eastern European in origin.*

MAKES 1 LOAF

2¼ cups unbleached white bread flour
Pinch of salt
1 tbsp fresh yeast
1 tbsp light brown sugar
⅓ cup milk, warmed
1 egg, beaten

Filling
1 egg
¼ cup ground almonds
½ cup poppy seeds, plus extra for
   decoration
½ cup raisins, soaked overnight
½ cup currants
½ candied cherries, chopped
¼ cup light brown sugar
¼ cup dates, chopped
Juice of half a lemon
Almond essence

¼ cup margarine
1 egg, beaten to glaze
¼ cup sliced almonds

1. Place the flour and salt in a bowl.

2. Cream the yeast and sugar together,
add the milk and stir well.

3. Add the beaten egg and leave for a few
minutes in a warm place.

4. Add the mixture to the flour and mix.
Knead well for 5 minutes.

5. Put into a clean bowl, cover and leave
to rise in a warm place for 40 minutes.

6. To make the filling, beat the egg,
reserving a little, and add all the other
filling ingredients. Mix well – the mixture
should be fairly moist.

7. To assemble, knock back the dough
and roll out to a rectangle 12 x 8 inches.

8. Dot half of the margarine over two
thirds of the dough from the top. Fold
over from the bottom to one third up,
then fold from top to bottom. Seal edges
and make one quarter turn.

9. Roll out to a rectangle shape again and
repeat with the remainder of the
margarine. Fold over as before but do not
roll out.

10. Place in the refrigerator for about half
an hour. Remove and roll out a rectangle
as before.

11. Cover with the filling, leaving a tiny
margin around the edges. Roll up width-
ways to make a fat sausage shape and
tuck in the ends. Brush with beaten egg.

12. Mark out in 1 inch slices, snipping
either side with scissors.

13. Sprinkle with the sliced almonds and
poppy seeds and leave to rise for a further
15 minutes.

14. Bake at 400°F for 30 minutes.

TIME: Preparation takes 25 minutes, cooking takes 30 minutes.
Proving takes 1 hour 40 minutes.

Soft Wheat Rolls

These may be split and toasted, buttered and then filled with cheese, eggs or vegetables to make a nutritious and satisfying snack.

MAKES 6

3 cups whole-wheat flour
1 tsp salt
2 tbsps fresh yeast
1 tsp brown sugar
¾ cup of milk
2 tbsps vegetable fat
1 egg, beaten

1. Put the flour and salt in a mixing bowl.

2. Cream the yeast and sugar together until liquid.

3. Warm the milk with the vegetable fat.

4. Mix the milk and fat with the creamed yeast and stir in the beaten egg.

5. Make a hollow in the flour and work the milk mixture in gradually to make a soft dough.

6. Knead about 10 minutes and form into six round rolls. Place on an oiled cookie sheet.

7. Cover and leave to rise for 20 minutes in a warm place.

8. Bake 425°F for about 15 minutes.

9. Glaze with beaten egg or milk a few minutes before removing from the oven.

TIME: Preparation takes 30 minutes, cooking takes 15 minutes.

VARIATION: Make Currant Cakes by adding ¾ cup currants and ¼ cup sugar to the recipe in the mixing.

WHOLE GRAIN ROLLS

*For a crisp crust, brush the rolls with salted water
and sprinkle with cracked wheat before baking.*

MAKES 10

3 cups whole grain flour
1 tsp salt
2 tbsps vegetable fat
1 tbsp fresh yeast or 2 tsps dried yeast
1 tsp brown sugar
1 cup warm water

1. Place the flour and salt in a mixing bowl and leave in a warm place.

2. Melt the vegetable fat in a pan and leave to cool.

3. Cream the yeast and sugar together with three-quarters of the warm water.

4. Make a well in the middle of the flour and pour in the yeast mixture.

5. Add the melted fat and mix to a pliable dough, adding the remaining water as necessary.

6. Knead lightly for a minute or two.

7. Cover with a clean tea towel and leave in a warm place until the dough has doubled in size.

8. Knead again for 3-5 minutes and shape into 10 smooth rolls.

9. Place well apart on a floured cookie sheet, cover and leave in a warm place until the rolls have doubled in size.

10. Bake in the center of a preheated oven, 425°F for 15-20 minutes or until the rolls sound hollow when tapped underneath.

11. Cool on a wire rack.

TIME: Preparation and rising takes 1 hour, cooking takes 15-20 minutes.

FREEZING: The rolls will freeze well for up to 1 month. Allow to thaw for 1 hour at room temperature before use.

SCOFA BREAD

The ideal chunky bread to serve warm with lunchtime salad meals.

MAKES 1 LOAF

5 cups whole-wheat flour
3 tbsps baking powder
2 cups bran
1 tsp salt
½ cup vegetable shortening
2¼ cups water
1 tbsp vegetable oil

1. Put the flour, baking powder, bran and salt into a mixing bowl.

2. Rub in the shortening and mix the water and oil together.

3. Make a well in the center of the flour and pour in the water and oil.

4. Mix in the flour, drawing it into the liquid mixture gradually from the sides, until a dough is formed.

5. Shape into a 7-inch round and place on a greased cookie sheet.

6. With a sharp knife cut to within ½ inch of the bottom, making four sections.

7. Bake just above the center of the oven, 400°F for about 1 hour or until nicely browned and hollow sounding when tapped with the back of your fingers.

8. Remove from the oven and wrap in a clean towel to cool.

TIME: Preparation takes 10 minutes, cooking takes 1 hour.

COOK'S TIP: Eat within a couple of days.

YOGURT SCONES

Serve with jam and cream for a traditional English teatime treat.

MAKES 10 SCONES

---

4 tbsps vegetable margarine or butter
2 cups wholemeal self-rising flour
2 tbsps demerara sugar
2 tbsps raisins
Plain yogurt to mix

---

1. Rub the fat into the flour and sugar.

2. Add the raisins and mix well.

3. Add enough yogurt to mix to a fairly stiff dough.

4. Knead the mixture lightly on a floured board and make two large circles of dough or cut into 2-inch rounds.

5. Bake in hot oven for 15-17 minutes at 425°F.

6. Remove and cool on a wire rack.

TIME: Preparation takes 10 minutes, cooking takes 15-17 minutes.

VARIATION: Use chopped dried apricots instead of raisins.

SOUP ROLLS

*These make an ideal accompaniment
for soup in place of bread.*

MAKES 6-8 ROLLS

2 cups whole-wheat flour
2 cups unbleached white flour
1 scant tsp salt
1 scant tsp baking soda
1 scant tsp cream of tartar
4 tbsps unsalted butter
1 egg, well beaten
⅔ cup plain yogurt
Milk

1. Preheat the oven to 425°F.

2. Sift the flours, salt, soda and cream of tartar twice and put into a mixing bowl.

3. Rub in the butter.

4. Put the yogurt into a large glass measuring cup and add milk. Stir well to make 1¼ cups.

5. Quickly stir the beaten egg into the flour followed by the yogurt and milk.

6. When the mixture has formed a soft dough, knead for a few seconds.

7. Divide the dough into 6 or 8 pieces and form into approximate rounds on an oiled cookie sheet.

8. Flatten the dough with your fingers.

9. Prick with a fork.

10. Bake for 8-10 minutes or until pale golden brown.

TIME: Preparation takes about 15 minutes, cooking takes 8-10 minutes.

VARIATION: Add ¼ cup of presoaked raisins or golden raisins.

369

OATLET COOKIES

*A delicious mix of oats, seeds and syrup
makes these cookies extra special.*

MAKES 10 COOKIES

1 cup oatmeal
1 cup all-purpose flour
¾ cup sunflower seeds
2 tbsps sesame seeds
½ tsp mixed spice
½ cup margarine
1 tbsp brown sugar
1 tsp molasses
½ tsp baking soda
1 tbsp boiling water
1¼ cups carob drops

1. Mix the oatmeal, flour, sunflower seeds, sesame seeds and spice together.

2. Melt the margarine, sugar and molasses over a gentle heat.

3. Add the baking soda and water to the syrup mixture and stir well.

4. Pour over dry ingredients and mix.

5. Place spoonfuls of the mixture well apart onto a greased cookie sheet and bake for 10 minutes at 375°F.

6. Allow to cool on the cookie sheet.

7. Melt the carob drops in a bowl over hot water and place teaspoonsful of the melted carob on top of the cookies. Leave to set. Store in an airtight tin.

TIME: Preparation takes 15 minutes, cooking takes 10 minutes.

VARIATION: Ground ginger can be used in place of the mixed spice.

COOK'S TIP: A bar of carob may be used in place of the carob drops.

MOLASSES OATIES

For a change try adding finely chopped nuts
or flaked coconut to this recipe.

MAKES ABOUT 20 COOKIES

½ cup margarine
½ cup brown sugar
1 tsp molasses
1 tsp boiling water
1 tsp baking soda
1 cup whole-wheat flour
1 cup oats
½ tsp baking powder

1. Melt the margarine, sugar and molasses in a saucepan.

2. Add the boiling water and baking soda.

3. Remove from the heat and stir in the flour, oatmeal and baking powder.

4. Place teaspoons of the mixture onto greased cookie sheets.

5. Bake at 325°F for 20 minutes.

6. Remove from the cookie sheets and place on a wire tray to cool.

TIME: Preparation takes 10 minutes, cooking takes 20 minutes.

VARIATION: Use ½ cup oatmeal and ½ cup flaked coconut, but reduce the amount of sugar slightly.

AMARETTI-ALMOND MACAROONS

Serve these delicious macaroons with tea or coffee.

MAKES ABOUT 24

2 cups whole blanched almonds
2 cups unrefined granulated sugar
2 egg whites
1 tsp almond extract

1. Grind the granulated sugar until fine.

2. Grind about ½ cup of the almonds at a time until very fine.

3. Sift the sugar and almonds together.

4. In a large bowl, beat the egg whites until stiff but not dry.

5. Gradually fold in the almond and sugar mixture and add the almond extract.

6. Spoon the mixture onto a floured cookie sheet, alternatively put the mixture on to sheets of edible rice paper.

7. Leave for as long as possible to rest before baking.

8. Preheat the oven to 350°F.

9. Bake for 15-20 minutes until pale golden brown.

10. Transfer the cooked macaroons to a cooling rack. Cool macaroons on rice paper until firm then trim around each leaving a circle of paper on the bottoms.

TIME: Preparation takes 15 minutes, cooking takes 15-20 minutes.

COOK'S TIP: The macaroons should be crisp on the outside but have rather chewy center. Longer cooking will crisp them all the way through if desired.

SHORTBREAD COOKIES

*Sandwich these biscuits together with
raspberry jam for a special treat.*

MAKES ABOUT 18

1¼ cups unbleached white flour
¼ cup light brown sugar
½ cup whipped margarine
½ tsp vanilla extract

1. Sift the flour and sugar together and rub in the margarine.

2. Add the vanilla extract and knead lightly to make a firm dough.

3. Form into small balls and place on a cookie sheet a few inches apart.

4. With the back of a fork, press the balls down making a criss-cross pattern.

5. Bake at 375°F for about 10-15 minutes until pale golden brown.

6. Cool and store in an airtight container.

TIME: Preparation takes 10 minutes, cooking takes 10-15 minutes.

VARIATIONS: Add a tablespoon of currants to make fruit cookies.
Omit the vanilla extract and substitute almond extract to make almond cookies.

Ginger Snaps

A great favorite with tea, coffee or hot chocolate.

MAKES 18-20

1 cup whole-wheat flour
1½ level tsps baking powder
1½ level tsps ground ginger
¼ cup soft brown sugar
Rind and juice of ½ lemon
3 tbsps corn syrup
¼ cup margarine

1. Sift the flour, baking powder, ginger and sugar into a mixing bowl.

2. Add the lemon rind and juice.

3. Melt the syrup and margarine over a low heat and stir into the dry ingredients.

4. Leave to cool.

5. Roll into small balls and place well apart on greased cookie trays.

6. Flatten out slightly with the back of a fork, still keeping their shape.

7. Cook at 375°F for 10-15 minutes.

8. Allow to cool for 2 minutes and then remove to a wire rack.

TIME: Preparation takes 10 minutes, cooking takes 10-15 minutes.

VARIATION: Substitute cinnamon for the ginger and sprinkle with chopped nuts.

COOK'S TIP: As the cookies cool they will become crisp. Store in an airtight tin.

OATMEAL CRUNCH

*If kept for a couple of days these bar
cookies turn deliciously soft and sticky.*

MAKES 24 SQUARES

1 cup butter or margarine
2 tbsps corn syrup
5 cups oatmeal
1 cup soft brown sugar

1. Put the butter and syrup into a pan and melt gently over a low heat.

2. Place the oatmeal in a large mixing bowl and mix in the sugar.

3. Pour over the melted butter and syrup and mix well with a wooden spoon.

4. Put the mixture into a greased 12 x 8 inch shallow cake pan and flatten well with the back of a spoon.

5. Bake in the centre of a 350°F oven for 30-35 minutes until golden brown on top.

6. Remove from the oven, allow to cool for 2-3 minutes and mark into squares.

7. Leave until nearly cold before removing.

8. Store in an airtight tin.

TIME: Preparation takes 10 minutes, cooking takes 30-35 minutes.

VARIATION: Use 3 cups of oatmeal and 2 cups of unsweetened muesli.

CHOC-OAT SLICES

Perfect for the lunch box or a kid's party.

MAKES 12 SLICES

4oz carob bar
½ cup hard margarine
1 tbsp clear honey
2 cups oatmeal
1 cup raisins
½ cup flaked coconut

1. Break the carob into a pan and add the margarine and honey.

2. Melt over a very low heat and stir until all the ingredients have melted.

3. Remove from the heat and add the oatmeal, raisins and coconut.

4. Spread the mixture evenly into a greased rectangular baking pan and bake at 350°F for 25-30 minutes.

5. Cool slightly and cut into slices.

6. When completely cold, remove and store in an airtight tin.

TIME: Preparation takes 10 minutes, cooking takes 25-30 minutes.

VARIATION: Chopped dates may be used in place of the raisins.
Try maple syrup instead of honey.

CAROB TRUFFLE BARS

Very rich and delicious bar cookies.

MAKES 16 SQUARES

2 cups graham crackers, broken up
½ cup margarine or butter
1 tbsp brown sugar
3 level tbsps carob powder
2 tbsps corn syrup
1 cup raisins
8oz carob bar

1. Crush the graham crackers finely with a rolling pin and place in a mixing bowl.

2. Put the margarine, sugar, carob powder and syrup into a pan and melt over a low heat, stirring all the time.

3. Add to the crumbs together with the raisins.

4. Mix very thoroughly.

5. Press the mixture into a 8 inch square pan.

6. Break the carob bar into a heatproof bowl and place over a pan of simmering water until melted.

7. Cover the cake with the melted carob and mark it with the back of a fork.

8. Refrigerate until cold.

9. Cut into squares and store in an airtight tin.

TIME: Preparation takes 20-25 minutes plus chilling time.

CARROT CAKE WITH APRICOT FILLING

This cake will freeze well for up to 2 months.

MAKES 1 CAKE

1 cup dried apricots
¾ cup butter or margarine
½ cup brown sugar
2 eggs, separated
1¾ cups all-purpose flour
1 tsp baking powder
½ cups carrots peeled and finely grated
½ cup raisins
¾ cup walnuts, finely chopped
2 tsps grated lemon rind
½ tsp ground cinnamon

1. Soak the apricots in water overnight, drain and purée until smooth.

2. Grease a 7-inch round spring mould pan or cake pan. Line the bottom of the pan with a circle of wax paper.

3. Beat the butter and sugar together until pale and creamy.

4. Whisk the egg yolks and beat into the butter and sugar.

5. Sift the flour and baking powder and fold into the mixture.

6. Add the rest of the ingredients except the egg whites.

7. Whisk the egg whites until they form soft peaks, and fold into the mixture.

8. Place the mixture in the greased tin and cook at 350°F for 45-50 minutes.

9. Cool in the tin for 10 minutes and then turn out onto a wire rack.

10. When completely cooled, slice in half and spoon the puréed apricot mixture onto the bottom half. Place the other half on top.

TIME: Preparation takes 20 minutes, cooking takes 45-50 minutes.

VARIATION: Replace the apricots with dried pears.

COOK'S TIP: This moist cake will sometimes crack on the top as it cools.

VIENNA CAKE

A versatile cake which can be adapted to suit any occasion.

SERVES 8-10

1 cup butter or margarine
1 cup Barbados or dark brown sugar
3 eggs, separated
3 tbsps milk
¾ cup carob powder
2 cups whole-wheat flour
6oz carob bar

1. Place the butter and sugar in a mixing bowl and cream together.

2. Add the egg yolks and beat well.

3. Mix in the milk.

4. Combine the carob powder with the flour and fold into the creamed mixture, which will be very stiff at this point.

5. Beat the egg whites until they are stiff and fold gently into the mixture.

6. Spoon mixture into a lined 7 inch pan and bake at 300°F for 1½ hours until a skewer inserted into the center comes out clean.

7. Turn out onto a wire rack to cool.

8. When the cake is completely cold, melt the carob bar in a bowl over a pan of simmering water.

9. Cover the cake with the melted carob, smoothing it with a knife dipped in boiling water.

10. Leave to harden before storing in an airtight tin.

TIME: Preparation takes 20 minutes, cooking takes 1½ hours.

SERVING IDEA: Serve with thickly whipped cream.

VARIATION: Instead of covering with carob, make into a layer cake by filling with cream and topping with fruit. For a richer cake add 1 cup of chopped walnuts to the basic mixture.

RICH FRUIT CAKE WITH GUINNESS

A deliciously moist fruit cake which is easy to make.

MAKES 1 CAKE

1 cup whipped margarine
1 cup dark brown sugar
4 medium eggs
2½ cups whole-wheat flour
2 tbsps mixed spice
4½ cups mixed dried fruit
10 tbsps Guinness or other stout

1. Cream the margarine and sugar together.

2. Beat in the eggs one at a time.

3. Gradually stir in the flour and mixed spice.

4. Mix in the dried fruit.

5. Add 4 tbsps Guinness to mix.

6. Spoon the mixture into a 7 inch spring form pan and make a deep well in the center, which will give the finished cake a flat top.

7. Cook for 1 hour at 325°F and then turn down to 300°F for a further 1½ hours.

8. Allow the cake to cool in the pan.

9. Remove and turn upside down. Prick the base of the cake all over with a skewer and slowly pour over the remaining 6 tbsps of Guinness.

10. Wrap and store in a cool place for at least a week before eating.

TIME: Preparation takes about 15 minutes, cooking takes 2½ hours.

SERVING IDEA: Serve at Christmas or other and special occasions. Accompany with chunks of cheddar cheese as they do in Northern England.

VARIATION: This mixture can be cooked in two 7½ x 4 inch loaf tins, reduce the final cooking time and cook until a skewer inserted into the cake comes out clean.

Banana Loaf

*Eat on its own as a cake or slice thinly and
butter to serve with tea or coffee.*

MAKES 1 LOAF

1 cup oatmeal
1 cup sugar
1 cup mixed fruit
1 cup banana-flavored soy milk
1 cup self-rising flour
Pinch of nutmeg

1. Prepare the cake the day before baking. Place all the ingredients except the flour and nutmeg into a large bowl and stir well.

2. Cover and put into the refrigerator overnight.

3. The following day, line or grease a 7½ x 4 inch loaf pan.

4. Mix the self-raising flour and the nutmeg gently into the mixture and put into the loaf pan.

5. Bake at 350°F for an hour or until a skewer inserted into the loaf comes out clean.

TIME: Preparation takes 10 minutes, cooking takes 1 hour.

VARIATIONS: ½ a tsp of mixed spice may be used in place of the nutmeg. Ordinary milk or plain soy milk can be used instead of banana soy milk.

COOK'S TIP: The loaf becomes more moist if left in an airtight tin for a day or two before eating.

PRUNE AND WALNUT LOAF

If you do not have prunes, dates taste just as good.

MAKES 1 LOAF

3 cups prunes
¾ cup water
3 cups fine whole-wheat flour
2 tsps baking powder
¼ cup brown sugar
1 tsp mixed spice
1 cup walnuts, chopped
4 tbsps sunflower oil
1 egg
Orange juice
Whole walnuts to decorate

1. Simmer the prunes in the water until soft.

2. Allow to cool, retain the cooking liquid, remove the stones and chop finely.

3. Mix the flour, baking powder, sugar, spice and walnuts together.

4. In a separate bowl mix the prunes, cooking liquid, oil and egg.

5. Fold together the flour mixture and the prune mixture, adding orange juice to give a soft consistency.

6. Put into a greased and lined 9 x 5 inch loaf pan.

7. Decorate with walnuts.

8. Bake at 325°F for 1¼ hours.

TIME: Preparation takes 15 minutes, cooking takes 1¼ hours.

FREEZING: Freeze after cooking for up to 2 months.

Fruit Cake

This cake freezes well.

MAKES 1 CAKE

3 cups whole-wheat flour
1 tsp mixed spice
1½ tsps baking soda
¾ cup margarine
¾ cup demerara sugar
1½ cups currants
¾ cup golden raisins
1¼ cups soy milk
1 tbsp lemon juice

1. Sift the flour, spice and baking soda together into a large bowl.

2. Rub in the fat until the mixture resembles fine breadcrumbs.

3. Add the sugar, currants and raisins.

4. Mix the milk and lemon juice together and add to the dry ingredients.

5. Mix well to form a dropping consistency.

6. Leave the mixture overnight.

7. Turn into a prepared 10 x 5 inch pan.

8. Bake in the center of the oven at 325°F for 2 hours.

TIME: Preparation takes 20 minutes, cooking takes 2 hours.

VARIATION: Use sour milk in place of the milk/lemon mixture.

OATMEAL AND MOLASSES SCONES

A tasty alternative to plain scones.

MAKES ABOUT 10 SCONES

1 cup whole-wheat flour
2 level tsps baking powder
Pinch of salt
2 tbsps margarine
1 cup oatmeal
1 tbsp molasses
Milk to bind

1. Sieve the flour, baking powder and salt into a bowl three times.

2. Rub in the margarine, then add the oatmeal.

3. Warm the molasses and 1 tbsp of the milk.

4. Bind the flour mixture with the molasses and milk, adding extra milk as necessary.

5. Roll out to 1-inch thick and cut into 2 inch rounds.

6. Bake on a greased cookie sheet at 425°F for 10 minutes.

7. Remove and place on a wire rack to cool.

TIME: Preparation takes 10 minutes, cooking takes 10 minutes.

FREEZING: The scones may be placed in a freezer bag or container and frozen after cooking.

INDEX